The Scientific Revolution

Other titles in the World History Series

WORLD HISTORY

The Scientific Revolution

Don Nardo

LUCENT BOOKS

A part of Gale, Cengage Learning

GALE
CENGAGE Learning

Detroit • New York • San Francisco • New Haven, Conn • Waterville, Maine • London

GALE
CENGAGE Learning™

LIBRARY OF CONGRESS CATALOGING-IN-PUBLICATION DATA

Nardo, Don, 1947-
  The scientific revolution / by Don Nardo.
      p. cm. -- (World history)
  Includes bibliographical references and index.
  ISBN 978-1-4205-0613-6 (hardcover)
  1. Discoveries in science--Europe--Juvenile literature. I. Title.
  Q180.55.D57N37 2011
  509.4--dc22
                                                              2011006556

Lucent Books
27500 Drake Rd.
Farmington Hills, MI 48331

ISBN-13: 978-1-4205-0613-6
ISBN-10: 1-4205-0613-7

Printed in the United States of America
1 2 3 4 5 6 7 15 14 13 12 11

Printed by Bang Printing, Brainerd, MN, 1st Ptg., 06/2011

Contents

Foreword

Each year, on the first day of school, nearly every history teacher faces the task of explaining why his or her students should study history. Many reasons have been given. One is that lessons exist in the past from which contemporary society can benefit and learn. Another is that exploration of the past allows us to see the origins of our customs, ideas, and institutions. Concepts such as democracy, ethnic conflict, or even things as trivial as fashion or mores, have historical roots.

Reasons such as these impress few students, however. If anything, these explanations seem remote and dull to young minds. Yet history is anything but dull. And therein lies what is perhaps the most compelling reason for studying history: History is filled with great stories. The classic themes of literature and drama—love and sacrifice, hatred and revenge, injustice and betrayal, adversity and overcoming adversity—fill the pages of history books, feeding the imagination as well as any of the great works of fiction do.

The story of the Children's Crusade, for example, is one of the most tragic in history. In 1212 Crusader fever hit Europe. A call went out from the pope that all good Christians should journey to Jerusalem to drive out the hated Muslims and return the city to Christian control. Heeding the call, thousands of children made the journey. Parents bravely allowed many children to go, and entire communities were inspired by the faith of these small Crusaders. Unfortunately, many boarded ships were captained by slave traders, who enthusiastically sold the children into slavery as soon as they arrived at their destination. Thousands died from disease, exposure, and starvation on the long march across Europe to the Mediterranean Sea. Others perished at sea.

Another story, from a modern and more familiar place, offers a soul-wrenching view of personal humiliation but also the ability to rise above it. Hatsuye Egami was one of 110,000 Japanese Americans sent to internment camps during World War II. "Since yesterday we Japanese have ceased to be human beings," he wrote in his diary. "We are numbers. We are no longer Egamis, but the number 23324. A tag with that number is on every trunk, suitcase and bag. Tags, also, on our breasts." Despite such dehumanizing treatment, most internees worked hard to control their bitterness. They created workable communities inside the camps and demonstrated again and again their loyalty as Americans.

These are but two of the many stories from history that can be found in the pages of the Lucent Books World History series. All World History titles rely on sound research and verifiable evidence, and all give students a clear sense of time, place, and chronology through maps and timelines as well as text.

All titles include a wide range of authoritative perspectives that demonstrate the complexity of historical interpretation and sharpen the reader's critical thinking skills. Formally documented quotations and annotated bibliographies enable students to locate and evaluate sources, often instantaneously via the Internet, and serve as valuable tools for further research and debate.

Finally, Lucent's World History titles present rousing good stories, featuring vivid primary source quotations drawn from unique, sometimes obscure sources such as diaries, public records, and contemporary chronicles. In this way, the voices of participants and witnesses as well as important biographers and historians bring the study of history to life. As we are caught up in the lives of others, we are reminded that we too are characters in the ongoing human saga, and we are better prepared for our own roles.

Important Dates at the Time

ca. 1600 B.C.
An Egyptian medical treatise advocates healing patients through a series of logical steps similar to those used by modern doctors.

ca. 600 B.C.
Greek scientists begin proposing rational explanations for nature's processes and mysteries.

ca. 200
Death of the brilliant Greek physician Galen, whose books will exert a major influence on early modern doctors.

476
The last Roman emperor is deposed, marking the end of the Roman Empire and ancient times.

600 B.C.	A.D. 200	500	800	1100

30 B.C.
Roman notable Octavian defeats his rivals, marking the end of the Roman Republic and start of the Roman Empire.

965
Birth of the great Muslim scientist Ibn Alhazen, later called the father of optics.

1215
In England, King John signs the Magna Carta, protecting the rights and privileges of his nobles.

384 B.C.
Birth of the Athenian scholar and thinker Aristotle, whose ideas will strongly influence early modern scientists.

of the Scientific Revolution

1620
English settlers establish a colony at Plymouth, in modern-day Massachusetts.

1682
Peter I, "the Great," becomes czar (emperor) of Russia.

1600
The Catholic Church burns scientist Giordano Bruno at the stake for his nontraditional views of the universe.

1543
Polish astronomer Nicolaus Copernicus publishes *On the Revolutions*, in which he advocates a sun-centered universe.

1776
Establishment of the United States by a group of individuals highly motivated by the principles of the Enlightenment.

1500	1550	1600	1650	1700

1578
Birth of English scientist William Harvey, discoverer of the circulation of blood in animals and humans.

1677
Scientist Robert Hooke manages to replicate Anton van Leeuwenhoek's microscopic observation of germs.

1704
English Enlightenment thinker John Locke, whose ideas will influence the U.S. Founding Fathers, dies.

1687
Newton publishes his *Principia*, setting forth his theory of universal gravitation and laws of motion.

1588
The English, under Queen Elizabeth I, defeat the Spanish Armada.

To Create a Better World

The Scientific Revolution was a series of scientific events and discoveries that occurred mostly in Europe in early modern times. Various historians of science date it somewhat differently. But in general terms, a majority of scholars agree that it transpired from about the mid-1500s to the mid-1700s, a period of roughly two centuries. The event most often cited for the start of the Scientific Revolution was Polish astronomer Nicolaus Copernicus's publication of *On the Revolutions of the Heavenly Spheres* in 1543. The book advocated the then radical idea that Earth and the other planets revolve around the sun. (Before that, the assumption was that all the heavenly bodies revolved around a stationary Earth.)

In contrast, no specific event marked the conclusion of the Scientific Revolution. The great English scientist Isaac Newton died in 1727, and most modern experts feel that in the two or three generations that followed, the Scientific Revolution blended into the enormous flood of new scientific discoveries that were made in Europe and elsewhere. As University of California scholar Margaret C. Jacob puts it, by the mid-1700s

> many educated people, especially in western and northern Europe, knew that Copernicus had been right and also knew that Isaac Newton's law of universal gravitation governed the motion of all the planets in relation to a stationary sun. [Also] no European or American colonial could be considered educated if he or she still believed that the earth stood still and in the center of the universe as the sun revolved around it.[1]

It is important to emphasize, however, that both the concept and dating of the Scientific Revolution are products of modern science. Copernicus, Newton, and their fellow thinkers had no notion that they were in the midst of a specific scientific era. In fact, the term "Scientific Revolution" was not coined until 1939 (by historian Alexandre Koyré), and its first use in a book title was in 1954. Thus, scholar Steven Shapin points out, the term was part of an effort by modern

Most historians consider the publication of Polish astronomer Nicolaus Copernicus's On the Revolutions of the Heavenly Spheres *in 1543 the start of the Scientific Revolution.*

science buffs to better understand scientific trends in past ages. He writes,

> The very idea of the Scientific Revolution [is] at least partly an expression of "our" interest in our ancestors. [We] want to know how we got from there to here, who the ancestors were, and what the lineage [succession of scientists] is that connects us to the past. [That] past is not transformed into the "modern world" at any single moment. We should never be surprised to find that seventeenth-century scientific practitioners often had about them as much of the ancient as the modern. Their notions had to be successfully transformed and redefined by generations of thinkers to become "ours."[2]

Why Did It Happen?

More important to modern scholars than when exactly the Scientific Revolution took place is *why* it happened when it did. One reason they often cite is that in the 1500s and 1600s the Roman Catholic Church was beginning to lose its iron grip on European minds and learning. For centuries the church had been Europe's most powerful and influential institution. In medieval times the pope and other church leaders, based in Rome, Italy, were in a very real sense the moderators of European social mores, including education and the ideas considered acceptable enough to be taught in schools. Those ideas were rooted mainly in the Bible. Priests, bishops, and other interpreters of that holy book strongly held that the sun moved around Earth, which lay at the center of the universe.

Over time, however, Europe's kings grew more powerful and began to challenge the church's authority. Also, in the early 1500s the Reformation, which witnessed the birth of numerous Protestant groups, shook the Catholic Church's foundations. As a result, the authority of the pope and bishops started to erode, especially among those thinkers who were on the cutting edge of science. In prior decades such men were sometimes arrested and/or burned at the stake for advocating ideas that contradicted biblical tradition. But increasingly, the church was unable to stop the onrushing tide of new scientific concepts. After all, "if something as venerable as the church could be questioned," Jacob writes, "might not other truths [about nature and world] bear scrutiny [inspection]?"[3]

Another reason that an upsurge in new scientific ideas occurred in the 1500s, 1600s, and 1700s was that in these years currents of social and political change were sweeping through Europe. Among these was the emergence of nonreligious, or nonchurch, centers of learning and scientific inquiry. In particular, scholars, thinkers, and serious students were attracted to the growing urban centers across the continent. There they found new universities teaching a wide range of subjects. Also, the royal courts in England, Belgium, the Netherlands,

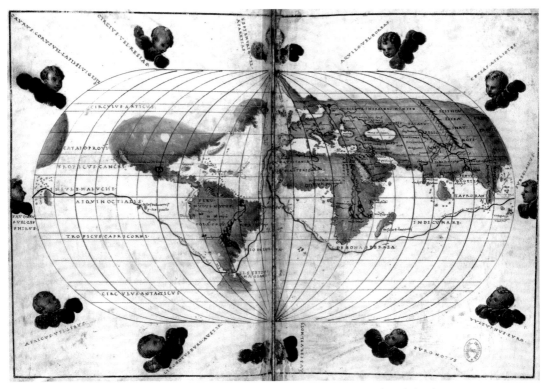

A period map shows Magellan's ships' route to circumnavigate the globe from 1519 to 1522.

western Germany, and parts of Italy offered money and other support for naturalists—thinkers interested in exploring and explaining nature's workings. Aiding in their work was the recently invented printing press, which provided a means of distributing new scientific ideas throughout Europe in only weeks or months. In prior ages, such ideas had taken years or even decades or more to become known to a majority of the population. In this way, printed books inspired new generations of young Europeans to study scientific concepts.

The Expansion of the World

Perhaps the biggest and most influential cause for the rise of modern science from the 1500s to the 1700s was the rapid expansion of the known world and the economic, social, and other changes it brought. Beginning in the late 1400s, European explorers sailed around the African continent and found North and South America. In addition, in 1522 the vessels originally launched by Spain's Ferdinand Magellan (who died on the voyage) returned from their historic journey around the world, the first ever.

These and other explorations across the globe opened up vast new trade routes, which allowed European kings, nobles, merchants, and bankers to grow rich. The voyages also stimulated the production of new inventions to make sailing and navigation more efficient and profitable.

"Above all," sociologist Robert K. Merton writes, such voyages "stressed anew the need for accurate and expedient means of determining [one's] position at sea." This involved the most efficient ways possible of finding longitude and latitude. Merton continues:

> Both mathematics and astronomy were [significantly] advanced through research oriented in this direction. [Isaac] Newton was likewise deeply interested in the same general problem. [His] lunar theory was the climactic outcome of scientific concentration on this subject. [Noted English astronomer Edmond] Halley, who had decided that various methods of determining longitude were all defective . . . constantly prompted Newton to continue his work. [Meanwhile, Halley himself] endeavored to rectify the lunar tables [records of the moon's movements] sufficiently to attain "the great object of finding the longitude with the requisite [necessary] degree of exactness." Observations of the eclipses of the moon were recommended by [other English scientists] for the same purpose.[4]

While astronomers, mathematicians, and others wrestled with finding better means of navigation, other researchers tried to find new and better industrial methods and more effective tools and weapons. Still others delved into the medical arts in order to help sailors stay healthy on long voyages. At the same time, geographers rushed to create more accurate maps, and inventors and machinists built more effective clocks, watches, and other instruments. In addition, huge amounts of new knowledge about other parts of the world poured into Europe. The discovery of new plant and animal species, as well as whole new civilizations of fellow humans, inspired numerous scientific discussions and theories among Europe's educated classes.

Broadening Horizons

Whatever the reasons for the onrush of the Scientific Revolution, once modern science was in full sway it could not be slowed or halted. In time it produced a more technically oriented and in many ways more comfortable world. Also, befitting Newton and the others who launched it, modern science continues to emphasize the idea that, given the time and the means, human beings can and will unravel the mysteries of nature and use that knowledge to create a better world. In the words of University of London scholar Lisa Jardine,

> The pursuit of science in the seventeenth century was an engaged, imaginative, and even adventurous affair. It brought together creative talents of all kinds, from all walks of life. [Science] galvanized [spurred into action] an entire continent, driving knowledge forward

at an astonishing speed. It broke down international barriers [and] broadened the horizons not just of the small circle of active [scientists] but of entire communities [and nations]. It heralded those everyday technologies that have allowed all of us, women and men alike, more or better opportunities to expand our individual understandings [of the world], increase our [life] experiences and [life expectancies], and, above all, learn [about the universe and our place within it].[5]

Chapter One

Forerunners of Modern Science

W hen Nicolaus Copernicus published his pivotal book proposing a heliocentric, or sun-centered, universe in 1543, European views about the nature of things did not change overnight. Indeed, at first few people read the book or were even aware of it. Even when scholars and other educated individuals did read and discuss it, many rejected Copernicus's ideas outright. They, along with almost everyone else in Europe, continued to accept the same traditional vision of nature and the universe their parents and grandparents had accepted. In that vision, Earth was a large sphere resting at the center of all things. Implicit in this geocentric, or Earth-centered, universe was the notion that the stars, planets, sun, and moon revolved around Earth, which was motionless.

Such popular prevailing views about the universe harkened back to the ancient Greeks. By late medieval times, a handful of Greek thinkers and scholars had come to be seen as nearly infallible sages, remnants of a lost intellectual tradition vastly superior to what came later. Among the most widely respected of these supposedly superior ancient authorities were Aristotle and Claudius Ptolemy (TAW-la-mee), both champions of the geocentric system.

The truth, of course, was very different, since Aristotle's and Ptolemy's vision of the universe turned out to be wrong. Nevertheless, they were proven to be right about a number of other things. More importantly, Aristotle and Ptolemy were part of the larger Greek invention of most of the scientific disciplines known today. The ancient Greeks therefore presented late medieval and early modern thinkers with a double-edged sword, so to speak. On the one hand, the work and ideas of Greek scientists made the modern scientific tradition possible. On the other, the major errors these thinkers made, which were perpetuated for centuries, had to be overcome before modern science could emerge. In large part, the Scientific Revolution was the process in which those mistakes were recognized and corrected.

Laying the Groundwork for Science

The Greek invention of science, which would eventually lead to the early modern Scientific Revolution, began in about 600 B.C. For countless centuries before that time, people everywhere, including

Copernicus's diagram and description of his sun-centered solar system from his 1543 book On the Revolutions of the Heavenly Spheres.

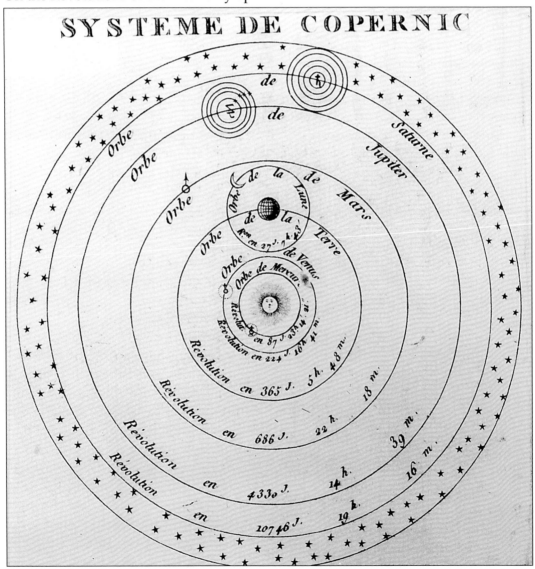

High Praise for Epicurus

The fourth-century B.C. Greek thinker Epicurus was a major supporter of the atomic theory proposed earlier by Democritus. The later Roman poet Lucretius praised Epicurus as an intellectual giant, saying in part:

When human life lay groveling in all men's sight, crushed under the dead weight of superstition . . . a man from Greece was first to raise mortal eyes in defiance, first to stand erect and brave the challenge. Fables and the gods did not crush him, nor the lightning flash and the growling menace of the sky. Rather, they quickened his manhood, so that he, first of all men, longed to smash the constraining locks of nature's doors. The vital vigor of his mind prevailed. He ventured far out beyond the flaming ramparts of the world and voyaged in mind throughout infinity. Returning victorious, he proclaimed to us what can be and what cannot. . . . Superstition, in its turn, lies crushed beneath his feet, and we, by his triumph, are lifted level with the skies.

Lucretius. *The Nature of the Universe.* Translated by Ronald Latham. New York: Penguin, 1994, p. 29.

Greece, thought that the universe, natural phenomena, and human destiny were all subject to the whims of various gods or other supernatural forces. The first Greek thinkers who are now seen as scientists rejected that concept. They viewed the universe as a rational, ordered place that worked according to underlying scientific principles. Furthermore, they said, humans possess the mental capacity to discover and explain those principles. "For the first time in history," scholar Rex Warner points out, it was assumed that "the investigator was dealing with a universe that was a 'cosmos'—that is to say an orderly system governed by laws which could be discovered by logical thought and by observation."[6] Thereafter, Greek scholars, as well as those from many other lands, often called the universe the cosmos, from which the words *cosmic* and *cosmology* derive.

Employing this new, rational approach to understanding nature, the first few generations of Greek scientists observed and discussed many diverse aspects of nature. Their efforts laid the groundwork for most of the major scientific disciplines, including astronomy, physics, chemistry, biology, mechanics, and medicine. At first, these disciplines were not viewed as separate subjects. Nor was science itself yet seen as separate from philosophy. So these early thinkers are often referred to as "philosopher-scientists."

The first of their number to have an impact on later scientific thought was Thales of Miletus (a large Greek city on the western coast of Anatolia, what is now Turkey). Like other early Greek philosopher-scientists he searched for what they called the *physis*, from which derive the modern terms "physical" and "physics." The Greeks defined it as nature's main underlying physical prin-ciple, or put more simply—what made nature tick. After much contemplation, Thales decided that the *physis* was water. Aristotle later wrote:

> Probably the idea was suggested to him by the fact that the nutriment of everything contains moisture, and that heat itself is generated out of moisture. [He] drew his notion also

Thales of Miletus was the first of the Greek philosopher-scientists to have an impact on later scientific thought.

from the fact that the seeds of everything have a moist nature. . . . The earth stays in place, he explained because it floats like wood or some such substance of nature to let it float upon water but not upon air.[7]

Other early Greek thinkers, including some of Thales's own students, suggested different substances for the *physis*. One of these students, Anaximander (born ca. 611 B.C.), held that nature's principal underlying material was an everlasting, invisible stuff he called the "Boundless." This substance, he said, somehow gave rise to the four chief elements that the Greek thinkers believed made up everything in the cosmos—earth, water, air, and fire.

Anaximander also tackled the mystery of the origins of life. He proposed that the first living creatures existed in the sea and that over time some of them crawled onto the dry land and adapted themselves to their new environment. Also, he said, humans came into being in a similar manner. A later Greek thinker named Empedocles (born ca. 493 B.C.) developed these concepts further. Before humans arrived on the scene, he stated, numerous and diverse species had existed. Some of them were not well adapted to survive in the harsh conditions they lived in, so they became extinct, and stronger, more flexible species took their place. A still later ancient writer summed up Empedocles's theory this way:

Monstrous and misshapen births were created, but all in vain. Nature debarred [prevented] them from [reproduction and survival]. Many species must have died out altogether and failed to reproduce their kind. Every species that you now see drawing the breath of life has been protected and preserved from the beginning of the world either by cunning or by prowess or by speed.[8]

For reasons unknown, Empedocles did not follow up on this evolutionary theory and attempt to collect a wide array of evidence to support it. Nor did any other ancient Greek scientist do so. More than two thousand years later, an English researcher, Charles Darwin, gathered the necessary evidence to support this same principle, which he called natural selection and others called "survival of the fittest." The fact that Empedocles stumbled on the truth so many centuries ago demonstrates that the ancient Greeks were every bit as smart as people are today. They simply lacked the inclination and/or resources to properly develop many of their ideas.

Other Inventive Theories

Greek scientists continued to produce a host of inventive, ingenious theories. Some are now known to be right or nearly so, while others were wrong but at least logical, honest attempts to explain nature's workings in physical terms. One of Empedocles's contemporaries, Anaxagoras (born ca. 500 B.C.), also advanced a theory to explain the origins of living things. It was based on his own explanation of the ever elusive

The Pythagoreans and Numbers

Pythagoras and his followers suggested that the physis *was made up of numbers, not material elements such as water. In other words, all objects in nature were shaped by and followed mathematical relationships. Also, these relationships harmonized, or were balanced, with one another. Aristotle later described the Pythagoreans' views, saying:*

They supposed that the elements of numbers were the elements of all the things that exist, and that the whole heaven was harmony and number. Everything in numbers and harmonies that cohered with [corresponded to] the properties and parts of the heavens and with the whole of the created world, they collected and fitted together. . . . The principles are ten in number and come in co-ordinate pairs: limit—infinite, odd—even . . . right—left, male—female [and so forth].

Aristotle. *Metaphysics,* quoted in Jonathan Barnes, ed. *Early Greek Philosophy.* New York: Penguin, 1987, p. 209.

Pythagoras and his followers believed the physis *was made up of numbers and that all objects in nature followed mathematical relationships.*

physis. Anaxagoras put forward the concept that the tiny "seeds" of all the tangible substances known to humanity exist deep inside all things. This somewhat puzzling notion was based partly on his observations of the act and consequences of eating. He pointed out that when people eat bread, fruits, and vegetables, they grow flesh, bones, skin, and hair. This could not occur, he said, unless the "seeds" of flesh, bones, skin, and hair were present in the food when it was eaten. How else, he asked, could hair come from something that was not hair in the first place? Thus, Anaxagoras proposed, "in everything there is a little bit of everything else. [And] that being so, we must believe that all this variety of things was present in the original whole."[9]

No less inventive was a theory advanced by the philosopher-scientist Pythagoras in the late 500s B.C. He and his followers, together called the Pythagoreans, held that the sky was composed of gigantic spheres nesting within one another. Moreover, the positions and movements of the heavenly spheres were all part of a single, perfectly tuned mathematical system. Like the strings of a harp, the spheres created harmonious musical effects.

The Pythagorean view of the heavens, like that of most ancient Greeks, was very much geocentric. A few Greek thinkers dissented from that view, however. One, Philolaus (born ca. 470 B.C.), correctly demoted Earth to the status of a planet. By contrast, he suggested that Earth, the other planets, and the sun all revolved around a "central fire" that was not visible from Earth. Aristarchus of Samos (born ca. 310 B.C.) actually got it right—that is, he claimed that Earth and the other planets went around the sun. Unfortunately for posterity, however, most of his writings did not survive, and a majority of Greek thinkers rejected his proposal of the heliocentric system.

Also rejected by many Greeks, though certainly not all of them, was the atomic theory. Leucippus and Democritus, both of whom lived in the 400s B.C., proposed that all matter is made up of tiny, invisible particles called atoms. But Aristotle (born 384 B.C.), who became by far the most influential of the Greek scientists, rejected the concept of atoms. So it never came into wide favor in ancient times. (Fortunately it at least survived, mainly in the writings of the Greek thinker Epicurus and the Roman philosopher Lucretius.)

The Perfection of God?

Meanwhile, Aristotle, who rejected the heliocentric view as well as atomism, built an enormous reputation as a philosopher-scientist. Much of this was for the immense strides he made in the fields of biology and zoology, including the creation of a very effective system for classifying animals. Aristotle also made many important educated guesses, some right and some wrong, about the nature of matter and the motion of material objects. However, by modern standards he would be seen as a very poor scientist, because he did not

Aristotle rejected the heliocentric view and was the first to create a system for classifying animals.

believe in experimentation. He and his followers "simply refused to test their ideas through doing experiments," astronomer John Gribbin remarks, "or to take any notice of the results of other people's experiments."[10]

Instead, one generation after another of later Greeks and Romans merely accepted Aristotle's views, sometimes building on them. The most important example was Ptolemy (born ca. A.D. 100), one of the chief astronomers of ancient times. In

Ptolemy Supports the Earth-Centered View

Claudius Ptolemy, whom later Europeans came to see as an astronomer and thinker of the highest order, worked at the Museum, a university in Greek-ruled Alexandria, Egypt. His greatest accomplishment was the Mathematike Syntaxis, *which later became known as the* Almagest. *A wide-ranging description of the heavens, it was built around the geocentric view that Aristotle had advocated earlier. Ptolemy held that his ideas were proven by direct observations of the sky. In this excerpt from his masterwork, he says that if Earth was not in the center of the universe, disaster would result.*

In brief, all the observed order of the increases and decreases of day and night would be thrown into utter confusion if the Earth were not in the middle [of the cosmos]. And there would be added the fact that the eclipses of the moon could not take place.

Ptolemy. *Almagest.* Translated by R. Catesby Taliaferro. Chicago: Encyclopedia Britannica, 1952, p. 10.

his main written work, the *Syntaxis*, now called the *Almagest*, he confirmed the geocentric view promoted by Aristotle. Ptolemy also listed the positions of 1,022 stars in forty-eight constellations, a sky map that remained in use in some places for the next fifteen centuries.

One unexpected twist came with the fall of the western Roman Empire in the fifth and sixth centuries A.D. Thereafter, Rome's main tongue, Latin, became *the* language of both the Catholic Church and scholarship. So at first a number of Latin manuscripts were preserved in Europe, while most Greek works in science and other subjects were set aside and forgotten. That included most of Aristotle's writings.

All was not completely lost, however. From the early 600s to roughly 1100, a flourishing Islamic culture burst from the Arabian Peninsula and spread across the Middle East, North Africa, and southern Spain. Muslim leaders encouraged learning and scientific inquiry. Moreover, educated Muslims eagerly read the ancient Greek scientific works, which had remained in circulation in parts of the Middle East, and translated many of them into Arabic. When the Muslims and Christians came into contact during the Crusades and later, these Arabic versions of the Greek manuscripts slowly but steadily filtered into Europe. There, they were translated once again, this time into Latin.

In this way, Aristotle, Ptolemy, and other Greek scientists came to be read and studied in Europe in late medieval times. Not only did these long-dead Greeks appear to be wise sages of a great and powerful past civilization, their staunchly geocentric views of the universe perfectly matched those of the Catholic Church. According to Gribbin, Aristotle's talk of "perfect" geometrical spheres in the heavens harmonized

> with the idea of the perfection of God and of God's works. So the whole kit and caboodle of Aristotelian cosmology . . . was swallowed up wholesale by the Catholic Church, with the implication that questioning any of this stuff was questioning the perfection of God, and therefore heresy.[11]

A Need for New Observation

Thus, by the early 1400s, in the midst of the European Renaissance, several ancient Greek scientists, especially Aristotle, had come to be seen as practically infallible sources of knowledge. Furthermore, the church enthusiastically endorsed these revered figures. So its hold over European society was stronger than it had ever been.

Yet even before the Scientific Revolution arose to openly challenge both Aristotle and the church, a few European thinkers had come to suspect something was wrong. In particular, they questioned the practice of accepting the authority of people long dead without testing their claims by experimenting and examining evidence. One of these questioners, Italian scholar Vincenzo Galilei, father of the famous Galileo Galilei, reportedly declared:

> It appears to me that those who rely simply on the weight of authority to prove any assertion, without searching out the arguments [i.e., the evidence] to support it, act absurdly. I wish to question freely and to answer freely without any sort of adulation [worship of scholars of past ages]. That well becomes any who are sincere in the search for truth.[12]

A group of Renaissance truth seekers known as the humanists were in full agreement with Vincenzo about the need for modern verification of ancient scientific claims. The term *humanist* derived from the Latin word *humanitas*, meaning "humanity." Men like the Italian Petrarch (born 1304) and the Dutch Desiderius Erasmus (born 1466) believed that it was important for humans to achieve their full potential, especially intellectually. They agreed with the ancient Greek philosophical argument that humans possess the intelligence required to uncover nature's hidden truths. There was no need to invoke divine or mystical authorities to discover such truths, they said. All that people needed to find these truths were the intellectual tools they already possessed—curiosity, reason, logic, and independent thinking.

It made no sense to Petrarch and the other humanists that people armed with such wonderful mental gifts regularly accepted the contents of centuries-old texts without question or independent verification. For one thing, most humanists worried about the accuracy of these texts. There had been no printing presses in ancient and early medieval times. So books and other writings were passed on by periodically copying them by hand. Errors were bound to be made,

Francisco Petrarch and other humanists believed that it was important for humans to achieve their full intellectual potential.

and these would be passed on to later copiers, who would make some mistakes of their own. Moreover, some humanists pointed out, the ancient texts had been translated numerous times from one language to another, a process that no doubt altered the meanings of many words and phrases.

It was therefore important to authenticate such texts, words, and phrases through observational science; that is, up-to-date testing and reexamination of evidence. Indeed, Steven Shapin says,

> the practice of humanistic literary scholarship commonly was closely joined to that of observational science. . . . Observation could help decide what the original text descriptions had actually been and, further, what ancient names and descriptions referred to what existing plants [or animals]. After all, wasn't this what the ancient authorities themselves had done? Hadn't Aristotle been a close observer of the natural world?[13]

The Business of Dirtying Hands

On the eve of the Scientific Revolution, therefore, at least some European thinkers were ready to reexamine and even to challenge the status quo of knowledge about the natural world. Also, the opening of the age of exploration showed that enormous numbers of formerly unknown lands, plants, animals, and peoples existed across the globe. This fantastic realization provided still more ammunition for re-thinking existing scientific knowledge. "Why had the ancient philosophers not foreseen the richness, complexity, and diversity that existed throughout the globe?" one modern scholar asks.

> Why is there no mention of the Americas in the Bible? [In] addition, travelers' encounters with Hindus, Muslims, and Jews—as well as the indigenous peoples of the New World—made it harder to assume that everything Western [i.e., European-based] must by definition be right or universal.[14]

These and other factors inspired a few intensely curious and brave Europeans to observe, question, and redefine the world rather than simply to accept what they had been told about it. According to Gribbin, they advocated testing various theories by getting their hands dirty while studying nature and the world, rather than simply discussing it as philosophers would. What these pioneers of modern science did not foresee was that their investigations of the world would, in the fullness of time, change it beyond their wildest imaginings.

Chapter Two

The Sun-Centered Universe

Most modern experts agree that the Scientific Revolution began when Nicolaus Copernicus published his *On the Revolutions of the Heavenly Spheres* in 1543. If it were possible for someone to travel back in time to that year, however, he or she would doubtless be disappointed. The time traveler would observe no uprisings or commotions of any consequence, either physical or intellectual. Life in Copernicus's homeland of Poland would seem no different than it had been in 1542. Moreover, if the traveler asked around, extremely few Poles would say they even knew who Copernicus was. Nor would they be aware that his book advocated the then controversial concept that the sun, and not Earth, lay at the center of the cosmos.

This seemingly peculiar situation illustrates that the revolution Copernicus started did not occur all at once. In fact, it was well more than a century and a half after the publication of his landmark book before large numbers of Europeans began to accept the heliocentric theory. The Copernican Revolution (an initial phase of the larger Scientific Revolution) was therefore very small-scale at first. Only a handful of scientists and churchmen debated, or even cared about, Copernicus's theory. However, among those scientists were some of the greatest early modern astronomers—Galileo, Tycho Brahe (TEE-koh BRAH-hee), and Johannes Kepler. They and a few others either championed the heliocentric system or brought it to the attention of a larger public. Its eventual acceptance by a majority of Europeans would mark a change in the way humans perceived the universe and their place within it.

A Passion for Astronomy

None of this was Copernicus's initial intention. Indeed, people who knew him when he was young could never have guessed that he would one day author a scientific theory that would rock the foundations of Western thought. Certainly they could not have conceived of his openly challenging the authority of the Catholic Church, then the spiritual and social guide for nearly all of Europe. Copernicus was raised as a devout Christian. Moreover, after his father died, when the boy was ten, his uncle, an influential bishop, made arrangements for him to study for a career in the church.

Yet Copernicus was too intellectually restless to commit himself to a job and life that perpetuated traditional customs and thinking. While attending Poland's Kraków University, he came under the wing of a professor of mathematics named Albert Brudzewski. The latter introduced the young man to the discipline of astronomy, which quickly became his passion. Copernicus's introduction to and preoccupation with the heliocentric view of the heavens occurred on his own time, however, and was not the result of influence from his professors. At the university, one of his modern biographers explains,

> he laid the foundations of his knowledge of [astronomy] and learned how to handle astronomical instruments and to make observations of the heavens. [But] he did not borrow his revolutionary ideas . . . from the public teachings and writings of [his masters]. The subject [of astronomy] was still taught

from the medieval point of view. That is, the movements of the heavenly bodies were still explained by reference to Aristotle's system of physics.[15]

One aspect of the astronomical theory put forth by Aristotle, Ptolemy, and other widely revered ancient Greeks seemed perfectly acceptable to Copernicus, as it did to other educated people of his day. This was the idea that Earth is spherical in shape. One strong piece of proof for this, Aristotle said, was the fact that Earth casts a curved shadow onto the moon during lunar eclipses. "How else would eclipses of the moon show segments shaped as we see them?" he asked in his essay "On the Heavens." Aristotle continued,

> As it is, the shapes which the Moon itself each month shows are of every kind—straight, gibbous, and concave—but in eclipses the outline is always curved. And, since it is the interposition of the earth [between the sun and moon] that makes the eclipse, the form of this line will be caused by the form of the earth's surface, which is therefore spherical. . . . Not only [is the earth] circular in shape, but also . . . it is a sphere of no great size. For otherwise, the effect of [a] slight change of place [i.e., traveling from one point to another on its surface] would not be so quickly apparent [in the way the constellations change position in the sky].[16]

Copernicus on Earth's Shape

In his landmark book, On the Revolutions of the Heavenly Spheres, *Copernicus offered huge amounts of mathematical and other evidence for the heliocentric theory. He began the work by stating some obvious characteristics of Earth and the heavens. In the following excerpt, for example, he gives some of the evidence proving Earth is a sphere.*

The earth is globe-shaped, [which] is made clear in this way. For when people journey northward from anywhere, the northern [point in the sky above] the [earth's] axis of daily revolution [by which he means rotation] gradually moves overhead, and the [southern point] moves downward to the same extent. And many stars situated to the north are seen not to set, and many to the south are seen not to rise anymore. So Italy does not see [the star] Canopus, which is visible to Egypt. . . . Conversely, for people who travel southward, [Canopus and other southern stars] become higher in the sky.

Nicolaus Copernicus. *On the Revolutions of the Heavenly Spheres.* Translated by Charles G. Wallace. Chicago: Encyclopedia Britannica, 1952, pp. 511–512.

Nicolaus Copernicus using his various instruments to study the night sky.

On these points—Earth's spherical shape and its relatively small size—Aristotle was correct. But another important aspect of his and Ptolemy's view of the cosmos was gravely in error. This was their contention that Earth rests, unmoving, at the center of the heavens. According to Aristotle (who agreed with the Pythagoreans on this point), the cosmos was made up of several large, invisible spheres that were concentric, or nested within one another. Attached to the surface of each sphere, he said, was a planet or other heavenly body. The sun rested on one sphere, the moon on another, Jupiter on still another, and so forth. Because these spheres were perfectly circular, they carried the heavenly bodies in perfect circles around the central Earth.

Simply Not Credible

The more thought Copernicus gave to this system of invisible concentric spheres, the more uncomfortable he became with it. Among his many objections was that to hold in place all of the heavenly bodies visible in the sky, there

Copernicus's heliocentric system, shown below, replaced Ptolemy's geocentric system, in which the planets were attached to the surfaces of invisible spheres, all encasing Earth.

would have to be an excessive number of these spheres, which would make the cosmos cluttered and unnecessarily complex. Also, the supposed movement of these spheres, along with the entire cosmos, around Earth every twenty-four hours was simply not credible in his view. For something so huge as the universe to attain this feat, he said, it would need to be moving at an unbelievably high speed. In addition, the Aristotelians claimed that "beyond the heavens there isn't any body or place or void or anything at all," in Copernicus's words. "And accordingly, it is not possible for the heavens to move outward. In that case, it is rather surprising that something [as immense as the heavens] can be held together by nothing!"[17]

It made much more sense to Copernicus for the opposite of the prevailing view to be true—that it was actually a tiny Earth that was moving within a huge, stationary cosmos. If so, he pointed out, the visual effect for humans would be identical to one that would result from the heavens moving around a stationary Earth. He asked,

Why, therefore, should we hesitate any longer to grant [Earth] the movement which accords naturally with its form, rather than put the whole [cosmos] in a commotion? [And] why not admit that the appearance of [the] daily revolution [movement] belongs to the heavens, but the reality belongs to the earth? . . . When a ship floats over a tranquil sea, all the things

outside [the ship] seem to the voyagers to be moving, [while] they themselves [seem to be] at rest. So it can easily happen in the case of the movement of the earth.[18]

It eventually became clear to Copernicus that Earth was moving through the cosmos in a circular motion. In his view, the visual and mathematical evidence indicated it was one of the planets, all of which were orbiting, or moving around, the stationary sun. "The sun is the center of the universe," he stated.

Moreover, since the sun remains stationary, whatever appears as a motion of the sun is really due rather to the motion of the earth. In comparison with any other spheres of the planets, the distance from the earth to the sun has a magnitude which is quite appreciable in proportion to those dimensions. But the size of the universe is so great that the distance earth-sun is imperceptible [extremely small] in relation to the sphere of the fixed stars. This should be admitted, I believe, in preference to perplexing the mind with an almost infinite multitude of [invisible] spheres, as must be done by those who kept the earth in the middle of the universe.[19]

Copernicus realized that he was not the first person to conceive of a heliocentric universe. In the 1400s a churchman, Nicholas of Cusa, had suggested that

The Catholic Church decided to ban Nicolaus Copernicus's book in 1616. Following is part of the decree issued by the church on March 5 of that year.

In regard to several books containing various heresies and errors, to prevent the emergence of more serious harm throughout Christendom, the Holy [Church] has decided that they should be altogether condemned and prohibited. . . . It orders that henceforth no one, of whatever station or condition, should dare print them, or have them printed, or read them, or have them in one's possession in any way [and] whoever is now or will be in the future in possession of them is required to surrender them to [the church's agents] immediately after learning of the present decree.

Quoted in "Galileo Trial Documents (1616)." http://my.pclink.com/~allchin/1814/retrial/1616docs.htm.

Earth moved through the heavens, and a few other scholars had said something similar. Furthermore, all of these late medieval researchers, including Copernicus, were aware that Aristarchus had proposed a heliocentric theory in ancient times. In fact, in an early draft of his *On the Revolutions*, Copernicus credited Aristarchus, and Philolaus too, with inspiring him, saying,

> It is likely that . . . Philolaus perceived the mobility [movement] of the earth, which also some say was the opinion of Aristarchus of Samos. [But] as these things are such as cannot be understood except by a sharp mind and prolonged diligence, it remained at that time hidden to most philosophers [ancient scientists], and there

were but few who grasped the reason of the motions of the stars.[20]

Yet among these forerunners of Copernicus and his views, none had presented any robust mathematical proofs for their claims. As scholar Thomas S. Kuhn points out, Copernicus was the first to accomplish that complex and impressive feat:

> The earth's motion [around the sun] had never been a popular concept [even when Aristarchus had proposed it in ancient times], but by the sixteenth century it was scarcely unprecedented. What was unprecedented was the mathematical system that Copernicus built upon the earth's motion. With the possible exception of Aristarchus,

Copernicus was the first to realize that the earth's motion might solve an existing astronomical problem or indeed a scientific problem of any sort. [He] was the first to develop a detailed account of the astronomical consequences of the earth's motion. Copernicus's mathematics distinguish him from his predecessors, and it was in part because of the mathematics that his work inaugurated a revolution [in scientific thought].[21]

Enter Bruno and Tycho

Unfortunately for Copernicus, he did not live long enough to see that revolution come to pass. He died in the same year his book was published, which affected the way scholars and other educated individuals viewed it. The fact that the author was not around to explain and defend its contents was one of the reasons it was so slow in changing Europe's intellectual landscape.

Even more influential in discouraging wide acceptance of Copernicus's expla-

A first edition of Copernicus's On the Revolutions. *Because Copernicus died the year it was published his theories were slow to gain widespread acceptance.*

nation of the heliocentric system was the Catholic Church. For a long time church officials had fervently backed the Aristotelian vision of the heavens because its geocentric system seemed to agree with various statements found in the Bible. So not surprisingly, any book that claimed the earth moved around the sun was bound to be seen as a threat to the church's credibility. Church astronomers therefore ridiculed and condemned Copernicus and his book. Several secular (nonchurch) astronomers did likewise, hoping to gain favor with society's most powerful and influential institution. Eventually the church went so far as to ban the book.

An unknown number of astronomers and other thinkers of the day agreed with Copernicus. But at first they chose to keep their real views private, fearing that the church would condemn, and maybe even punish, them if they came out in support of the heliocentric system. Among these secret Copernicans was the young Italian scientist Galileo. In 1597 he admitted his true feelings on the matter to the brilliant German astronomer and mathematician Johannes Kepler, who also agreed with most of Copernicus's ideas. Galileo wrote that he had "not dared until now to bring" his acceptance of the heliocentric theory "into the open," because he feared suffering the same fate as "Copernicus himself," who had been "derided and dishonored."[22]

That Galileo had made the right choice in remaining silent became all too apparent three years later. In 1600

Dominican friar Giordano Bruno escaped the Inquisition and fled to England where he wrote two treatises supporting Copernicus's heliocentric theory.

the church dealt drastically with an Italian scientist who had gone public with his support for Copernicus's views. This brave soul was a former Dominican friar named Giordano Bruno. In the early 1580s he had moved to London, where the church could not have him arrested (because England had recently broken away from the Catholic Church and become Protestant). There, he had published two treatises supporting the heliocentric theory—*The Ash Wednesday Supper* and *On the Infinite Universe and Worlds*. These works made some logical, but at the time radical, leaps based on Copernicus's ideas. One stated that not only was Earth a planet, there were also planets orbiting other stars and there might even be intelligent creatures living on those faraway planets. He wrote,

> Our world, called the terrestrial globe, is identical as far as material composition goes with the other worlds, the [orbiting] bodies of other stars. [And] it is childish to . . . believe otherwise. [Also] there live and strive on [those distant planets] many and innumerable [beings] to no less extent than we see these living and growing on the back of this [earth]. Aristotle and others are blinded so as not to perceive the motion of the earth to be true and necessary. They are, indeed, so inhibited that they cannot believe [earth's motion through the heav-

Galileo's Fear of Going Public

In 1597, Galileo wrote a letter to noted German astronomer Johannes Kepler to explain why he had not gone public with his support of the heliocentric theory.

Like you, I accepted the Copernican position several years ago and discovered from thence the causes of many natural effects which are doubtless inexplicable by the current theories. I have written up many of my reasons and refutations on the subject, but I have not dared until now to bring them into the open, being warned by the fortunes of Copernicus himself . . . who procured immortal fame among a few but [by most has been] derided [ridiculed] and dishonored. I would dare publish my thoughts if there were many like you; but, since there are not, I shall forebear [hold back].

Quoted in Galileo Galilei. *Le Opere di Galileo Galilei*. Vol. 10. Edited by Antonio Favaro. Florence, Italy: G. Barbera Editrice, 1968, p. 68.

ens] to be possible. But once this is admitted, many secrets of nature, hitherto hidden, do unfold.[23]

Church officials desperately wanted to silence Bruno for publicly stating what they claimed were heretical, or highly sacrilegious, views. But as long as he stayed in England or other Protestant lands, he was safe from their wrath. In 1591, however, he committed a foolhardy and grave error. Keeping a low profile, he paid a visit to the Italian city of Venice, where a man he thought was his friend reported his presence to local church officials. Bruno was arrested, imprisoned in Rome, and tried as a heretic. When he continually refused to abandon his views about the heavens, agents of the church burned him at the stake on February 17, 1600.

Bruno's sad fate demonstrated that it was not yet safe for most European thinkers to publicly support the heliocentric theory. However, that did not mean one could not challenge Aristotle. In 1588 the ingenious Danish astronomer Tycho Brahe showed that there was a middle ground—a way to say that Aristotle had erred without contradicting the Bible and angering the church. In the Tychonic model, named for the man who invented it, all of the planets except for Earth revolved in perfect circles around the sun. Meanwhile, the sun moved, carrying those bodies with it, around a stationary Earth. Sure enough, church leaders had few gripes about Tycho's cosmic view because it was essentially geocentric and therefore no threat to prevailing religious beliefs.

Danish astronomer Tycho Brahe's model of the planets had all of the them, except for Earth, revolving around the sun while the sun revolved around Earth.

Kepler and His Laws

Quite unknowingly, however, Tycho made it possible for the Copernican system, which he had rejected, to eventually triumph. This happened because the aging Tycho had heard good things about a young German mathematics teacher, Johannes Kepler, and offered him a job. Over the course of two decades, the older man had closely observed the planets and collected an enormous mass of facts and figures about their motions. He was confident that careful studies of this data would show the shapes of the planets' orbits and thereby prove the

Tychonic model was correct. Kepler's assigned task, which began in the winter of 1599–1560, was to use complex mathematical formulas to make sense of the collected data.

But things did not work out the way Tycho expected and wanted. First, he grew ill and died in October 1601. That left Kepler in the midst of decoding the data. The work continued for several years, during which the young math whiz tried over and over to make Tycho's figures match the perfect circles he and other scientists assumed for the planetary orbits. But no matter how hard he tried, the data simply did not match such orbits.

Then it suddenly hit Kepler that he and all his predecessors, including Copernicus himself, might have been deluding themselves. What if the orbits of the planets were not circular, but elliptical, or oval-shaped? Sure enough, when Kepler plugged Tycho's data into elliptical orbits, everything matched precisely.

In 1609 Kepler published the first two of his three planetary laws. The first one says that the planets travel in elliptical orbits around the sun. The second law states that a planet picks up speed as it nears the sun and slows down as it moves away from it. As a result, an imaginary line connecting a planet to the sun sweeps out equal areas in equal amounts of time.

A few years later, Kepler announced his third law, which relates a planet's period, or the time it takes to orbit the sun, to its distance from the sun. Because Mars is farther from the sun than Earth is, Kepler

In 1609 Johannes Kepler published his first two planetary laws: the first, that the planets followed elliptical orbits, and the second, that a planet picks up speed as it nears the sun and slows down as it moves away.

said, Mars moves more slowly than Earth and therefore has a longer period. Because Kepler's laws showed how the planets' visible movements could be explained in terms of their revolving around the sun, they provided extremely persuasive proof for the heliocentric theory. In addition, they perfectly explained the moon's orbit around Earth and even the orbits of all the comets that had been observed by astronomers up to that time.

Kepler was certain that his findings would revolutionize astronomy, in part by showing that Copernicus was right.

In his 1619 book *Harmony of the Worlds*, Kepler wrote: "It is fitting that we accept with grateful minds this gift from God, and both acknowledge and build upon it. [This] will lead us along a path to the reform of the whole of astronomy." His mention of God indicated that he remained a devout Christian. However, he had become convinced that God had fashioned a sort of "clockwork universe," a vast machine-like unit that operated on physical, mathematical, provable principles. "The machinery of the heavens is not like a divine animal," he said, "but like a clock."[24]

In spite of the mathematical evidence Kepler had provided, however, the Copernican Revolution was not yet complete. The church, along with a number of scientists who dared not defy its authority, continued to resist the heliocentric system. This was partly because the math Kepler had employed was tremendously complex and understandable to only a handful of people. What was needed was a kind of proof everyone could easily comprehend and appreciate. Even before Kepler's death, in 1630, a new invention—the telescope—was beginning to provide that proof. The question was whether those who were most resistant to intellectual change would believe the evidence of their own eyes.

Chapter Three

An Eye on the Sky: The Telescope

Well after Copernicus published his masterwork and Kepler formulated his laws of planetary motion, astronomy, the study of the heavenly bodies, remained one of the leading branches of the Scientific Revolution. For one thing, the battle between the geocentric and heliocentric theories was still raging. Also, even among those who embraced the sun-centered view, there was still much debate over the true nature of the cosmos.

In many quarters, however, there was hope that the development of a powerful new scientific tool might stop the battles and settle the debates. This instrument, the telescope, gave humans a proverbial eye on the sky. For the first time, they could see beyond the paltry limits imposed by their naked eyes and view formerly invisible cosmic worlds. Moreover, there was widespread agreement that the initial scopes were small and that in time much larger ones would be built that would allow astronomers to see farther into space. Surely these would expand knowledge of the universe and Earth's place within it even further. As Steven Shapin puts it,

From the early seventeenth century, observers using telescopes . . . suggested that revelation of even more details and more marvels [in the heavens] only awaited improved instruments. . . . Who could confidently say what did and did not exist in the world when tomorrow might reveal as yet undreamed-of inhabitants in the domains of the very distant? [In part because of the telescope] the traditional expression of the limits of knowledge, *ne plus ultra*—"no farther"—was defiantly replaced with the modern *plus ultra*—"farther yet."[25]

For some scientists and other observers, the telescope possessed seemingly miraculous powers to reveal heavenly truths. People should believe the evidence of their own eyes, they said, and learn from it, no matter which traditional views of nature might be swept aside. Certainly that was the view expressed by the telescope's first great practitioner, Galileo. To his regret and sadness, however, he learned that some traditions die particularly hard. At first the church refused to accept the evidence the telescope provided and punished Galileo severely for trying to perpetuate the ongoing Scientific Revolution. His fateful story reveals how the first great hurdle in that revolution's path was overcome.

The Power of the Eye

One reason that the church was able to hold back the momentum of the Scientific Revolution as long as it did was the excellence of Europe's pre-telescope astronomers and the intellectual authority they wielded. Today, many people are

An astronomer uses an early wooden telescope to observe the planets circa 1673.

unaware of the impressive strides these individuals made before Galileo turned his telescope toward the sky. Their discipline, now referred to as "naked-eye astronomy," went back thousands of years to the ancient Babylonians, Persians, Greeks, and Chinese, as well as the medieval Arabs.

The astronomers of those cultures enjoyed the benefit of observing in velvety-black, crystal-clear skies unhindered by the industrial and light pollution that limits naked-eye observations of the sky today. As a result, people with unusually good vision were able to see objects in the night sky that can be perceived only in binoculars and small telescopes today. They closely watched those objects, especially the sun, moon, planets, and comets, which moved slowly through the fields of fixed stars. They also kept detailed records of these movements.

By Europe's last few medieval centuries, naked-eye astronomy had reached a remarkable level of technical sophistication. Kings and well-to-do nobles poured large amounts of money into building and supporting observatories where astronomers employed a wide array of instruments to observe the heavens. This trend reached its height in Denmark in the sixteenth century. There, in 1576, King Frederick II agreed to give the brilliant Danish thinker Tycho Brahe all the material and financial backing he required for his work. Tycho acquired a castle equipped with a large observatory, along with dozens of assistants and servants. These facili-

ties were located on the island of Hven, not far off Denmark's western coast. Frederick told Tycho: "There you can live peacefully and carry out the studies that interest you, without anyone disturbing you. [You] are said to have considerable insight into [the nature of the heavens]. I see it as my duty to support and promote something like this."[26] By modern standards, the king did more than his duty. He actually gave Tycho the island and everything on it to exploit in any manner he saw fit!

The observatory on the island had a large central room filled with books, star charts (globe-like models of the heavens), and many mechanical instruments. Among the latter was an armillary. (The armillary was invented before Tycho's time. But his versions of it were larger and much more accurate than those that preceded him.) Shaped like a sphere, it consisted of several large, movable metal rings with numbers painted onto their edges. These numbers represented the 180 degrees (each degree consisting of sixty minutes) into which the visible sky was divided. By moving the armillary's rings in various ways and sighting along them, Tycho and his assistants were able to measure the positions of stars and planets at any given time and with amazing precision. One of the armillaries Tycho built was 10 feet (3m) across and could measure star positions to within 1/120 of a degree, an incredibly tiny margin of error for an instrument guided solely by the naked eye.

The tremendous level of scientific achievement that was possible with

This period print shows the grounds of Tycho's castle observatory on the Isle of Hven.

instruments as good as Tycho's, along with a mind as brilliant as his, was demonstrated in 1577. On the evening of November 13, he saw a bright object in the western sky that he immediately realized did not belong there. It was fuzzy looking and had a faint tail. Clearly, Tycho reasoned, the object was a comet. He vigilantly watched it move across the sky from night to night until it vanished from view in January 1578.

After carefully studying the measurements his instruments had made of the object, Tycho became perplexed. The comet appeared to have been located well beyond the moon, at a distance of about 1.2 million miles (1.9 million km) from Earth. But how could this be, he wondered? Aristotle had insisted that comets always move inside Earth's atmosphere. Moreover, Tycho's instruments had indicated that the comet was orbiting the sun, and Aristotle had said that all heavenly bodies, including the sun, move around Earth. In this way, using only naked-eye observations, aided by some ingenious instruments, Tycho was able to disprove Aristotle. The Danish astronomer's observations of the comet of 1577 became his main

Tycho's Quadrants

The great naked-eye astronomer Tycho Brahe employed numerous ingenious instruments to aid him and his assistants in observing the night sky and measuring the positions of the heavenly bodies. Among these devices were quadrants he designed himself. At the time, a quadrant measured the altitude of a star or planet from the

horizon. It was an apparatus with a wooden or metal framework shaped like a large pizza slice and covered 90 degrees, or a quarter of a full circle, hence the meaning of the term *quadrant* — "one-quarter." To use one of his quadrants, Tycho sighted two distant objects through holes on the device's rim and measured the angle between them. The degree of accuracy he achieved in doing this often amazes people today. One of his quadrants measured star positions with an error of only thirty-two seconds of arc. That amounts to just 1/120 of a degree.

One of the quadrants Tycho used to measure the altitude of a star or a planet from the horizon.

motivation in constructing the Tychonic model of the cosmos, in which all the heavenly bodies except Earth orbited the sun, while the sun moved around Earth.

The Earliest Telescopes

Tycho's reputation as a brilliant astronomer and a thinker practically on a par with Aristotle and other ancient sages spread throughout Europe. In the 1570s and 1580s, it appeared to most people, including church leaders, that astronomy had reached its greatest possible height. Indeed, in this view no astronomical instruments would ever surpass those Tycho had built, and no further major discoveries about the universe seemed likely.

Partly because of this shortsighted thinking, most of the initial telescope-makers did not even think to use the instrument to study the sky. Those that did, moreover, made the unfortunate decision to keep such studies secret. So their findings were lost to the march of science. Several of these inventors worked independently across Europe in the late 1500s and early 1600s. So it appears that no single person can be credited with inventing the telescope.

Possibly the first of these instruments were built by English mathematician and surveyor Leonard Digges (born 1520). Remarks made later in the letters of his son, Thomas, and others who knew him suggest that the elder Digges fashioned two or more scopes sometime in the 1550s. Furthermore, evidence implies that they were of both initial telescope types—refractors and reflectors. (Other kinds of scopes, some of which combine elements of refractors and reflectors, did not begin to appear until the 1800s.) A refractor creates a magnified image by passing light through two convex lenses, that is, lenses that are thicker in the middle and thinner toward the edges. A reflector creates a similar image by bouncing light off of a concave mirror, one that is slightly bowl-shaped. (In Digges's era, the word "telescope" had not yet been coined. So experts on optics, the study of the behavior of light, referred to refracting scopes as "perspective glasses" and called the mirror of a reflecting scope a "plain glass.")

The strongest single piece of evidence for Digges's scopes is an official English government report made circa 1580. Evidently Leonard and Thomas Digges decided to keep their telescopes a secret. The reasons for this are unclear. It may be that they feared others would steal the design, causing them to lose both control of the invention and any profits that might accrue from selling it. In any case, word of the scopes leaked out. Eventually, a major adviser to Queen Elizabeth I heard a rumor that the Digges family had a device that made faraway objects appear to be closer. Appreciating the military potential of such an instrument, the adviser sent an agent named William Bourne to see if there was any truth to the rumor. Bourne's surviving report, though sketchy and a bit hard to follow, seems to describe both reflecting and refracting telescopes:

[I will describe] the effects of what may be done with these last two sorts of glasses [scopes]. The one concave with a foil upon the hilly side [i.e., a concave mirror, having a reflecting foil on the back] and the other ground and polished smooth, the thickest in the middle, and thinnest towards the edges [a double-convex lens]. I am assured that the glass that is ground, being of very clear stuff, and of good largeness, and placed so that the [light] beam does come through, and so received into a very large concave looking glass, that it will show the thing of marvelous largeness, in a manner incredible to be believed of the common people.[27]

It appears that the scopes built by Leonard Digges either remained hidden or no longer existed by the 1580s. However, by that time, spectacle, or eyeglass, makers in various parts of Europe were experimenting with lenses in ways that made the independent invention of the telescope inevitable. (These craftsmen had been using convex lenses to help people with vision problems since the late 1200s.) One spectacle maker, a Dutchman named Hans Lippershey, tinkered together a small, crude, but workable refractor by the early months of 1608. It consisted of two convex lenses, later called the objective and secondary lenses. The objective lens collected incoming light and bent, or refracted, it, focusing it into a small image. The secondary lens, which Lippershey placed in front of the objective, magnified the image, making it look larger and closer.

To Lippershey and his associates, the small scope, which he called a "spyglass," was at first viewed mainly as a novelty. He made several models of it, and some ended up at parties thrown by well-to-

Leonard Digges's Telescopes

The following tract was written in the 1570s by English researcher Thomas Digges. Some experts say he described some crude telescopes built earlier by his father, Leonard Digges. Although not certain, it appears that both refracting and reflecting scopes are mentioned here.

[I begin by describing] the effects of a plain glass [reflective mirror]. Marvelous are the conclusions that may be performed by glasses concave [mirrors] and convex [lenses] of circular and parabolic forms, using for multiplication of [light] beams sometime the aide of glasses transparent, which by fraction [refraction] should unite or dissipate the images or figures presented by the reflection of the other. By these kind of glasses or rather frames of them, placed in due angles, you may not only set out before your eye the little image of every town, village, etc . . . you shall discern any trifle [small thing], or read any letter there lying open, especially if the sun beams [sunlight] come unto it, as plainly as if you were [standing beside them], although [they] be distant from you as far as [your] eye can [see]. [These are] the miraculous effects of perspective glasses [telescopes].

Quoted in Gilbert Scatterthwaite. "Did the Reflecting Telescope Have English Origins?" www.chocky. demon.co.uk/oas/diggeshistory.html.

Dutch spectacle maker Hans Lippershey put together two convex lenses to make his early telescope, the spyglass.

do Dutch, who marveled at how it made faraway houses and other objects seem much closer. Eventually, Lippershey, like Queen Elizabeth's adviser, realized that his device might also have military applications, including allowing commanders to see enemy fleets and armies approaching from a great distance. Late in 1608, therefore, he gave the invention to the Dutch government.

Enter Galileo

What Lippershey evidently did not appreciate was that rumors about his spyglasses, spread by partygoers and others who had seen them, had already made it across Europe. Hearing about a magical image-inflating device made with lenses, several smart, mechanically inclined individuals immediately set to work experimenting with lenses and building their own scopes. Among them were an Italian, Paolo Sarpi, and an Englishman, Thomas Harriot.

Another clever Italian, Galileo Galilei, heard about the Dutch invention in July 1609. Putting everything else aside, he hurriedly obtained some convex lenses and began trying them out in various combinations. Although he had never seen an example of Lippershey's spyglass, he instantly grasped the principle involved. So within a few days he was able to create a telescope that magnified ten times. (In other words, it made a faraway object look to be ten times closer than it actually was.) This early scope magnified images about as well as an

These two telescopes are replicas of the ones Galileo built and used to make observations of the planets and their moons.

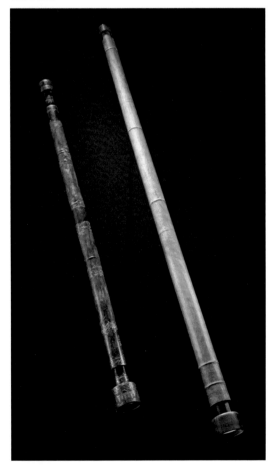

average pair of modern binoculars. Galileo took the instrument to Venice and demonstrated it for the members of that city's well-known senate, who immediately recognized its military potential. The demonstration was also intended to establish Galileo as a major telescope-builder and cutting-edge astronomer.

The Venetian senators, along with nearly everyone else who had built or seen previous telescopes, had completely overlooked the device's potential for viewing the moon, planets, and other objects in the sky. Being an astronomer, however, Galileo readily appreciated this potential. As soon as he returned home from Venice, where he had given his first scope to that city's leader, he built a new instrument that magnified twenty times and trained it on the moon. To his delight, he saw that it was covered with craters, mountains, and what appeared to be seas. (Later astronomers discovered that instead of bodies of water, these *maria*, plural of the Latin *mare*, meaning "sea," are actually large plains of dust.)

Barely able to contain his excitement, Galileo pointed the scope at various spots in the Milky Way, the long band of pale light that ripples through several constellations. The instrument revealed that seemingly solid smudge in the night sky to be made up of countless numbers of individual stars, nearly all of them too distant to see with the unaided eye. Switching to the planets Venus, Jupiter, and Mars, Galileo saw globes that looked like the moon, only smaller (because they are much farther from Earth than the moon is).

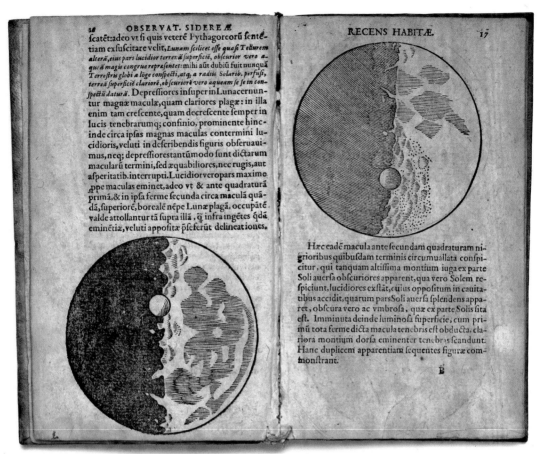

In Galileo's book The Starry Messenger, *he showed that his observations of Earth's moon had revealed craters, mountains, and valleys. Also, the moon was not perfectly smooth and spherical as previously thought.*

Even more important, for both astronomy and the Scientific Revolution, was something Galileo saw near Jupiter's globe. At first he thought they were four distant stars that happened to lie in the planet's present line of sight. But as he observed them over the ensuing nights, he saw that they moved. Not only that, the movement was not random, but showed that the four objects were orbiting Jupiter, exactly as the moon revolves around Earth. Realizing that he was seeing Jupiter's own moons, Galileo imme-

diately grasped the momentous implication this discovery had for the ongoing Copernican Revolution. Scholar James MacLachlan explains,

Aristotelians had argued that the earth was the center of the universe because everything seemed to revolve around it, and no other object was the center of any rotations. Now, with moons in orbit around Jupiter, that argument was clearly invalid.[28]

An Eye on the Sky: The Telescope ■ 49

Plainly, Galileo realized, Earth was not the center of all things, as both the ancient sages and the church's leaders had long thought. The geocentric theory was therefore erroneous. In Galileo's mind, the proof for this major assertion was now incontrovertible, or unarguable. The telescope provided tangible evidence that anyone, even someone with no scientific background at all, could see as conclusive. Thus, he reasoned, he no longer had to fear what the church would do when its leaders found out about his astronomical views. They would have no choice but to believe the evidence of their own eyes and alter their views about the cosmos accordingly.

Based on this reasoning, Galileo compiled his telescopic discoveries in writing and published them in a sixty-page booklet in March 1610. It was titled *The Starry Messenger*. Its author was thrilled when the Latin edition of the book rapidly sold out and was subsequently translated into numerous other languages, including Chinese. Soon Galileo was famous throughout the known world. This notoriety also brought him both prestige and job offers in his native Italy. Cosimo II, Grand Duke of Tuscany, appointed him to the post of First Mathematician of the royal court, and Galileo also accepted the post of chief mathematician at the University of Pisa (in northern Italy).

A New Vision of the Future

Galileo's joy eventually turned to distress, however. His assumption that church officials would be persuaded to change their views about the heavens based on what the telescope had revealed turned out to be wrong. In fact, to his astonishment he found that many people both inside and outside the church would not accept the telescopic evidence. Some even refused to look into the device. "What would you say of the learned [Italians] who [have] steadfastly refused to cast a glance through the telescope?" Galileo asked in a letter to Kepler. "What shall we make of all this? Shall we laugh or shall we cry?"[29]

Those church officials who did look through the telescope and saw Jupiter's moons told Galileo that this and other so-called evidence the instrument had revealed proved nothing. It all could be explained, they said, using Tycho's vision of the heavens, which was geocentric. Further, in 1616 they warned Galileo not to write anything else suggesting the Copernican theory might be correct.

Eight years later, the disgruntled astronomer met several times with Pope Urban VIII in Rome. Galileo walked away from the meetings with the impression that he could write about the Copernican view as long as he said it was only a hypothesis. Then he got to work on a major treatise titled *Dialogue Concerning the Two Chief World Systems*, which he finished in 1629. At first, the church's censors cleared the book for publication. But not long after it was released to the public, the church reversed itself, halted further publication, and ordered Galileo to stand trial on suspicion of heresy.

Galileo Recants His Heliocentric Views

Following is part of Galileo's abjuration, his public admission that he had been in error in advocating ideas that were hostile to the church's views.

I must altogether abandon the false opinion that the sun is the center of the world and immovable, and that the earth is not the center of the world, and moves, and that I must not hold, defend, or teach in any way whatsoever, verbally or in writing, the said doctrine, and after it had been notified to me that the said doctrine was contrary to Holy Scripture—I wrote and printed a book in which I discuss this doctrine already condemned, and adduce arguments of great cogency in its favor . . . and for this cause I have been pronounced by the Holy Office to be vehemently suspected of heresy. . . . Therefore, [I] abjure, curse, and detest the aforesaid errors and heresies. [And] I swear that in the future I will never again say or assert, verbally or in writing, anything that might furnish occasion for a similar suspicion regarding me.

Quoted in Galileo Galilei. *Le Opere di Galileo Galilei.* Vol. 19. Edited by Antonio Favaro. Florence, Italy: G. Barbera Editrice, 1968, p. 406.

The proceedings did not go well for the aging scientist. In 1633 he was found guilty and forced to publicly renounce the heliocentric theory. After this humiliation, he endured the constraints of house arrest until he died in 1642, a broken and unhappy man.

In the long run, however, Galileo was vindicated. In the century following his passing, science, including the discipline of astronomy, advanced rapidly. It became clear that the heliocentric view of the cosmos was correct, a fact proven in part by continuing advances in optics and telescope making. Refractors got larger and larger and rendered increasingly sharp images, which clarified various cosmic mysteries. For example,

Galileo's small, relatively crude scope revealed Saturn as a fuzzy blob with weird bumps protruding from its sides. But in 1655, Dutch astronomer Christiaan Huygens observed Saturn with a larger, more refined instrument that magnified fifty times. It showed that the bumps Galileo had seen were the outer edges of that planet's magnificent ring system.

Meanwhile, other scientists experimented with new telescope designs, including ways of building effective reflectors. This work culminated in the late 1600s with the construction of a working reflector by English researcher Isaac Newton, considered one of the most brilliant individuals to have ever lived.

In 1669 he wrote to a friend, "I have seen with it Jupiter distinctly round and his satellites."[30] Newton proceeded to create a second reflector, which he gave to the recently formed Royal Society, a group of scientists dedicated to the advancement of knowledge. That advancement continued and accelerated as telescopes became larger and more sophisticated. In the late 1700s German-born English astronomer William Herschel built several large reflectors and with one of them discovered Uranus, the first new planet found since ancient times.

By Herschel's day, the Scientific Revolution had wrought enormous changes in the way people viewed the universe, nature, and the quest to better understand both. The arrogant old notion—that nothing new about the heavens would ever be found—had been swept away. In its place rested a much more optimistic vision of the future, in which the discoveries made by the human mind, aided by increasingly effective technology, would be virtually limitless. Christopher Wren (born 1632), the famous English architect who was also an astronomer and physicist, summed it up elegantly, saying,

A time [will] come, when men should be able to stretch out their eyes . . . by which means they should be able to discover *two thousand* times as many stars as we can [today], and find the Galaxy to be [made up of] myriads [large numbers] of them. And every nebulous star appearing as if it were the firmament [sun and sky] of some other world [like Earth], at a . . . distance [from us too far for us to calculate], buried in the vast abyss of [the limitless] vacuum [of space].[31]

Chapter Four

The Scientific Method Advances

During the Scientific Revolution, while Galileo and other early modern scientists were arguing about the nature of the universe, they were also developing a workable scientific method. They saw that, like all human endeavors, science required a practical approach. A military general who wanted to create an army went about it using tried-and-true methods. Similarly, a potter approached making a bowl by employing the same general, practical steps that other potters did. A scientific method was therefore a set of general rules for scientific investigation.

The problem for scientists during much of the Scientific Revolution era was that no such set of rules was accepted by everyone. Various ancient scholars, including Aristotle, had proposed ways of approaching the acquisition of knowledge. Some medieval thinkers had done the same, and among the scientists of Galileo's age each had his own prefer-

ences for how to conduct research. What made the Scientific Revolution important in this respect was that over hundreds of years several of the best ideas about scientific methodology came together. In a way, they crystallized into a generally accepted approach to scientific research that, with a few minor alterations, is still in use today.

Early Attempts at a Method

A major part of the process of creating a viable scientific method during the 1500s, 1600s, and 1700s was looking back on what earlier thinkers had done and either keeping or rejecting their ideas and approaches. It was (and still is) difficult to tell who had been the first person to propose a version of the scientific method. It could well be that several people did so independently in different places and times. Perhaps the earliest known example was the unknown author of an ancient Egyptian medical

Learning from Existing Knowledge

Aristotle believed that one of the first and most basic steps in making correct statements about nature or the world was to study what others had said before on the subject. From that, one could see what the consensus is and use it as a starting point in forming one's own opinion on the matter. In the opening of his Posterior Analytics, *he said:*

All teaching and all intellectual learning come about from already existing knowledge. This is evident if we consider it in every case, for mathematical sciences are acquired in this fashion, and so is each of the other arts. And similarly, too, with arguments, [which] produce their teaching through what we are already aware of, [getting] their premises [principles] from men [teachers, philosophers, etc.] who grasp them.

Aristotle. *Posterior Analytics,* in Jonathan Barnes, ed. *The Complete Works of Aristotle.* Vol. 1. Princeton, NJ: Princeton University Press, 1984, p. 114.

book now known as the *Edwin Smith Papyrus.* Dating from about 1600 B.C., it advocated that a doctor follow a series of logical steps in trying to heal a patient. These included examination, diagnosis, treatment, and prognosis. This organized method for dealing with disease is nearly identical to the one used by modern physicians. (It should be noted that not all Egyptian doctors followed this process. Numerous other approaches to healing existed in ancient Egypt, many of which relied on superstition rather than logic.)

When Galileo and other researchers of the Scientific Revolution were born, the chief method of assessing new knowledge was the one created by Aristotle in the fourth century B.C. Aristotle held that all knowledge could be traced back to a basic and eternal set of "first principles."

These were fundamental truths about nature that need not be questioned, he said. One could infer their existence through beliefs that had long existed, supplemented by assumptions based on observation.

For example, based on simple observation it appeared that the heavenly bodies moved around a stationary Earth. So it seemed only right that Earth should be the center of all things, and that fact could be accepted as a first principle. Another first principle derived from a general belief in higher powers. Most people accepted that the heavenly system called the cosmos had been created by a god or gods, and it seemed to make no sense for a divine being to fashion a faulty system. Therefore, it could be accepted that the universe operated on perfect principles. One such principle was that the moon and other heavenly bodies followed perfectly circular paths around the earth. Moreover, any new proposal that contradicted such first principles was deemed incorrect.

Aristotle also held that various scientific principles could be derived through logic, for which he devised a complex system. It utilized a method called a syllogism, which operates by comparing one thing to another and making conclusions based on that comparison. One of Aristotle's many examples (in his *Posterior Analytics*) is as follows: "If A belongs to every B in what it is [i.e., in its nature], and B is said universally of every C in what it is, necessarily A is said of C in what it is."[32] Aristotle called A the major premise, B the minor premise, and C the conclusion.

A practical example of such a syllogism would be: A, all people breathe; B, all children are people; therefore, C, all children breathe. Syllogisms can be used in other ways as well, Aristotle said. For instance, if A does something, and B does not do that thing, then the conclusion, C, is that A is not B. A practical example would be: A dog barks; and a goat does *not* bark; therefore, a dog is not a goat (or dogs and goats are two different things).

In all his talk of first principles and defining things through syllogisms

The earliest known example of an attempt at the scientific method was described in this Egyptian medical papyrus from around 1600 B.C.

The World Has Changed

Francis Bacon acknowledged that ancient thinkers like Aristotle had contributed much to human knowledge. But he felt that their ideas should not always be automatically accepted without further testing, because the world had changed a great deal since their day. In his Great Instauration, *written in 1620, Bacon said:*

We have no reason to be ashamed of the discoveries which have been made, and no doubt the ancients proved themselves in everything that turns on wit and abstract meditation, wonderful men. But, as in former ages, when men sailed only by observation of the stars, they could indeed coast along the shores of the old continent or cross a few small and Mediterranean seas; but before the ocean could be traversed and the new world discovered, the use of the mariner's needle [compass], as a more faithful and certain guide, had to be found out; in like manner . . . before we can reach the remoter and more hidden parts of nature, it is necessary that a more perfect use and application of the human mind and intellect be introduced.

Francis Bacon. *The Great Instauration.* Edited by James Spedding et al. Boston: Taggard and Thompson, 1863. Available at: www.constitution.org/bacon/instauration.htm.

and other logic, Aristotle emphasized the power of observation and reason to make scientific and other conclusions. But he did not advocate experimentation, nor did most other Greek thinkers. As scholar H.D.P. Lee explains, this was a fundamental drawback to their scientific method:

The comparative failure of the Greeks to develop experimental science was due to many causes. . . . They lacked instruments of precision—there were, for instance, no accurate clocks [and] they did not produce until a comparatively late date any glass suitable for chemi-

cal experiment or lens making. Their iron-making technique was elementary, which precluded the development of the machine. Their mathematical notation was clumsy and unsuited to scientific calculation. All these things would have severely limited the development of an experimental science had the Greeks fully grasped its method. But the experimental method eluded them.[33]

Enter the Arabs

Indeed, Western thinkers did not begin to recognize the value of experimentation in science until late medieval times. Until recently, most textbooks in the West failed to mention that these scholars were influenced by medieval Arab scientists who preceded them by several centuries. Beginning in the 800s, well before the works of Aristotle and many other Greeks were rediscovered in Europe, Muslim scholars translated these treatises into Arabic. At the Academy of Wisdom in Baghdad (in what is now Iraq), then a major center of learning, Muslim scholars wrote commentaries on the Greek books.

Inspired by these works, the Muslim scholars went on to produce a burst of scientific accomplishments of their own. For example, a mathematician named al-Khwarizmi introduced what came to be called Arabic numerals, based on an Indian number system. Because of their simplicity, they made mathematical calculation considerably easier than it had been in the past. Arabic numerals filtered into Europe beginning in the late 900s and subsequently improved the methodology of scientists across Asia and Europe.

Arab Muslim scholars made many other contributions to science, including in the disciplines of medicine, chemistry, geography, astronomy, and cartography (mapmaking). Perhaps the greatest of these were the achievements of Ibn Alhazen (or al-Haythem), who was born in 965 in Basra, in what is now Iraq, and educated in Baghdad. He dabbled in several areas, but his main interest was the behavior of light. The first person to correctly describe how

people see objects, today he is universally recognized as the father of the science of optics. According to one modern researcher,

He proved experimentally that the so-called emission theory (which stated that light from our eyes shines upon the objects we see), which was

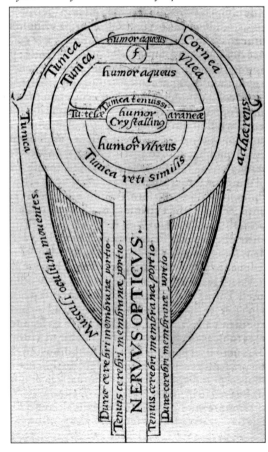

Arab scientist Ibn Alhazen's diagram of the human eye in his book Opticae Thesaurus. *He studied the behavior of light and its effect on the eye and is universally credited with being the "father" of the science of optics.*

believed by great thinkers such as Plato, Euclid and Ptolemy, was wrong and established the modern idea that we see because light enters our eyes. What he also did that no other scientist had tried before was to use mathematics to describe and prove this process.[34]

Another crucial contribution Alhazen made to science was to formulate a scientific method containing the concept of experimentation. Closely familiar with Aristotle's works, he greatly respected the Greek's abilities and accomplishments. But Alhazen recognized that Aristotle had proven his assertions only verbally, which meant that they could be endlessly challenged by other theories. In contrast, performing experiments could show which theory was true and which was false or at least less true. The result, as researcher Martyn Shuttleworth tells it, was that Alhazen

developed a scientific method very similar to our own: 1. State an explicit problem, based upon observation and experimentation. 2. Test or criticize a hypothesis [suggested explanation] through experimentation. 3. Interpret the data and come to a conclusion, ideally using mathematics. 4. Publish the findings. Ibn Alhazen, brilliantly, understood that controlled and systematic experimentation and measurement were essential to discovering new knowledge.[35]

The Method Continues to Evolve

In the 1100s, some of Alhazen's texts, a few by other Arab scientists, and works by Aristotle and other Greeks that had been lost to the West since Rome's fall became known in Europe. Interest in them was so strong that they were fairly rapidly translated into Latin, the language used most often in the writings of thinkers and other literate people. Among the first Europeans to be strongly influenced by them was English friar and philosopher Roger Bacon (born 1214).

Among many accomplishments, Bacon played an especially prominent role in the evolution of the scientific method. Impressed by Alhazen's ideas on methodology, he promoted the use of experimentation along with observation and logical deduction. In a work appropriately titled *On Experimental Science*, Bacon stated:

There are two ways of acquiring knowledge, one through reason, the other by experiment. Argument reaches a conclusion and compels us to admit it, but it neither makes us certain nor so annihilates doubt that the mind rests calm in the intuition of truth, unless it finds this certitude [certainty] by way of experience. Thus many have arguments toward attainable facts, but because they have not experienced them, they overlook them and neither avoid a harmful nor follow a beneficial course. Even if a man that has never seen fire, proves by good reasoning that fire burns, and devours and destroys things, nevertheless the mind of one hearing his arguments would never be convinced, nor would he avoid fire until he puts his hand or some combustible thing into it in order to prove by experiment what the argument taught. But after the fact of combustion is experienced, the mind is satisfied and lies calm in the certainty of truth. Hence argument is not enough, but experience is.[36]

Later, during the Scientific Revolution, another Englishman, Francis Bacon (born 1561; no relation to Roger), also advocated the use of performing experiments as part of scientific research. First, Bacon discarded the idea of accepting

A page from Roger Bacon's On Experimental Science *shows the English philosopher and scientist at work in his study. Drawing on Alhazen's methodology, Bacon advocated the use of experimentation with observation to draw logical deductions.*

first principles about nature based on assumptions, a process that Aristotle had routinely used. Instead of relying on assumed knowledge, Francis Bacon said, one should start with observation, then move to gathering as many unbiased facts as possible about the thing being observed. Next, one should study these facts diligently and if possible draw from them one or more preliminary conclusions, or hypotheses. Finally, he said, one should devise experiments to test

Francis Bacon believed in observation combined with the gathering of unbiased facts and scrutinizing them to draw a hypothesis. He then devised an experiment to test that hypothesis.

those conclusions. If the tests showed a conclusion was wrong, the researcher should go back to the facts and draw a new one.

Another important early modern contributor to the scientific method was French mathematician, physicist, and philosopher René Descartes (born 1596). He viewed the natural world and the phenomena within it as a big collection of mechanical objects, like a giant machine, all carefully manufactured by God. Further, Descartes proposed, God had purposely designed these machine parts so that they could be explained by humans using mathematics. The single exception was the human mind (or soul), which Descartes claimed was separate from mechanical things and endowed with a divine spark.

As for the method Descartes suggested for investigating God's vast cosmic machine, he partly echoed Aristotle. One should begin with reason and logic rather than observation, Descartes declared. However, first one should break down the problem at hand into several smaller parts; this is because understanding each part will better allow the investigator to make an overall conclusion about the whole. About this process, called reductionism, he said:

> Divide each of the difficulties [to be examined] into as many parts as would be possible and as would be required in order better to resolve them. [Then] conduct [one's] thoughts in such an orderly manner that by beginning with objects

French mathematician, physicist, and philosopher René Descartes wrote that the natural world (and all phenomena within it) was a big collection of mechanical objects—a giant machine carefully manufactured by God.

that are the simplest and easiest to know, [one] might ascend little by little—as it were step by step—to the knowledge of the more complex.[37]

Francis Bacon and Descartes advocated reaching final conclusions in different ways. But parts of each of their methods were both valid and useful, so modern science combined their approaches. Today it is standard procedure in science to observe; reduce the thing to be studied into small, manageable parts; draw preliminary conclusions; and perform experiments to verify them.

Experimental Evidence Is Preferable

A few other researchers during the Scientific Revolution independently adopted the use of experimentation to test their hypotheses. The most famous was Galileo. Following his death, a story circulated widely that he had staged an experiment to refute one of Aristotle's statements about motion. The ancient Greek had asserted that objects of different weights fall at different rates; specifically, heavier ones fall faster than lighter ones. Galileo knew that Aristotle had not tested this hypothesis through experimentation—by physically dropping objects of varying weights—and suspected he was wrong. Galileo was certain that all objects, regardless of weight, would fall at the same rate. That much of the story is true.

However, the part of the story in which Galileo dropped cannonballs of varying weights off the Leaning Tower of Pisa to test this suspicion is *not* true. The experiment was actually performed in 1612 by an Italian professor who was trying to show that Aristotle was right. When dropped simultaneously, the larger ball beat the smaller ball to the ground by two inches, which prompted the professor to say that Galileo's criticism of Aristotle was wrong.

Making an Informed Estimate

Like many other scientists, Galileo used induction, the process of drawing conclusions based on a specific set of observations. He rightly recognized that his final conclusion would have to be only an "informed estimate" because of all the variables involved in most natural systems. Researcher Martyn Shuttleworth elaborates:

[Galileo] understood that no empirical evidence could perfectly match theoretical predictions. He believed that it would be impossible for an experimenter to take into account every single variable. In the world of physics, for example, Galileo theorized that mass had no effect upon gravitational acceleration. No experiment could ever hope to measure this perfectly, because of air resistance, friction, and inaccuracies with timing devices and methods. However, repetition by independent researchers could build up a body of evidence that allowed an extrapolation [estimation based on observations] to the general theory to be made.

Martyn Shuttleworth. "History of the Scientific Method." www.experiment-resources.com/history-of-the-scientific-method.html.

In reality, however, the experiment proved Galileo was right! Many years later, in his *Discourses and Mathematical Demonstrations Relating to Two New Sciences* (1638), Galileo recalled the experiment. According to Aristotle, the larger object should have fallen twice as fast as the smaller one. Yet as Galileo reminded his readers, the objects landed at nearly the same time. The tiny difference, he said, was attributable to the effects of air resistance, which were more pronounced on the smaller object. (In 1971, when Apollo 15 astronaut Dave Scott stood on the moon's surface, he simultaneously dropped a hammer and a feather. Because the moon has no air, there was no air resistance, and sure enough, both objects touched the ground at exactly the same time.)

Francis Bacon's and Galileo's promotion of the use of experimentation to supplement observation and reason strongly influenced other scientists of their generation and those that followed. In the 1660s, the newly formed Royal Society followed their lead. That prestigious organization took the position that experimental evidence was always superior and preferable to theoretical evidence. Not long afterward, Isaac Newton (born 1642), the greatest early modern scientist, reaffirmed the main elements of sound scientific methodology. They included careful observation and fact-gathering, forming hypotheses based on observed facts, and testing the hypotheses through experimentation. In this way, by the end of the Scientific Revolution (in the mid-1700s), the modern scientific method had emerged.

Chapter Five

The Revival of Medical Research

One of the most important and influential developments of the Scientific Revolution was the renewal of serious medical research in Europe. Exploration for knowledge about the human body and the causes and cures of disease had remained at a virtual standstill since about A.D. 200, roughly three centuries before the end of the ancient era. That was the approximate date for the death of the great Greek physician Galen. He had been born circa 130 and had pursued vigorous medical research in the same period in which Claudius Ptolemy had produced his famous treatises on geography and astronomy.

An extremely gifted and hardworking scholar, Galen became the leading medical practitioner of the Roman Empire. In part this was because he collected and studied the works of the finest Greek doctors of the past. One expert observer writes, "Galen's merit is to have crystal-lized or brought to a focus all the best work of the Greek medical schools which had preceded his own time."[38] Another reason that Galen's work was so influential was that he performed numerous experiments of his own, including dissecting pigs, dogs, and other animals. He also wrote many books, about eighty of which have survived, detailing the best medical knowledge of his time.

No Greek or Roman medical doctor or researcher after Galen came close to his level of scientific achievement. For that reason, his books had a profound impact on later European scholars and thinkers. As in the case of the works of Aristotle and other Greeks, after Rome's fall these books were at first translated into Arabic and studied by Muslim scientists. Shortly before the Renaissance, however, they were rediscovered in Europe and Galen quickly came to be seen as a nearly infallible sage. The prevailing view was that no new medical research was necessary, because, as scholar John Gribbin says, Galen's ideas were "like some kind of holy writ that could never be improved."[39]

Only with the onset of the Scientific Revolution did this situation begin to change. "Soon one man, Andreas Vesalius," Gribben continues, "was questioning the accuracy of Galen's teaching and taking anatomy, in particular, further."[40] Vesalius's anatomy students, and later their own pupils, continued to take up the torch of medical research that he had lit. Aiding them and others in the medical community was an exciting new investigative tool—the microscope. It made possible many momentous new discoveries, including the existence of germs, which would eventually have huge consequences for humanity.

New Approaches to Anatomy

Vesalius, a Belgian, was born in 1514. After studying anatomy in Paris, France, in 1537 he journeyed to Padua, in northern Italy, to complete his education. There, he witnessed doctors doing dissections of human corpses, something that Galen had not been able to do (because the laws of his time prohibited it). When Vesalius started doing his own human dissections, he quickly concluded that human anatomy was improperly and inaccurately taught, not only in Paris and Padua, but across Europe. Gribbin explains:

The teaching (such as it was) was based on the assumption that Galen was right, and that the purpose of the dissection was to point out the truths he had laid down. The professor in charge of the dissection would read the relevant passages [from Galen's books], while a surgeon (in those days, a very lowly member of the [medical] pecking order) carried out the actual dissection, and a third member of the team, called an ostensor, would use a pointer to indicate the various organs and so on being referred to by the professor. The idea was simply to demonstrate what was already known, and *had* been known since Galen's time.[41]

When Vesalius started teaching anatomy, he used a different approach. He did the dissections for his students himself and explained the significance of each step, rather than referring to Galen's writings. This method was so effective that it began to spread to other Italian universities and later to some in other countries. Vesalius proceeded to make important discoveries about the structure of the heart, nervous system, and muscles. Also, in 1543, the same year that Copernicus published his masterwork advocating the heliocentric system, Vesalius published *On the Fabric of the Human Body.* In it, he strongly advocated that physicians and medical researchers do their own human dissections and come to their own conclusions without relying on what the ancient authors said.

Vesalius's influence remained strong well after he stopped teaching in Italy,

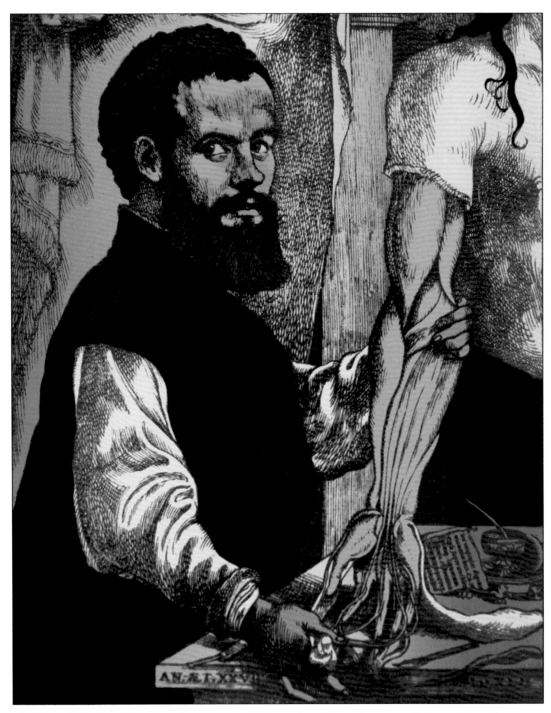

Andreas Vesalius dissects a human arm. He used a different approach to anatomy by doing the dissections himself while explaining to his students the significance of each step in the process.

as well as after he died in 1564. One of his students at Padua, Gabriele Fallopio (or Fallopius), started teaching anatomy there in 1551 and became famous for discovering the human fallopian tubes (in the female reproductive system). Fallopio's own student, Girolamo Fabrizio, also carried on Vesalius's methods and was professor to one of the greatest medical researchers of all time, William Harvey.

Circulation of the Blood

Harvey, who was born in England in 1578, got his medical degree in Padua in 1602 and later taught anatomy and surgery at London's Royal College of Physicians. In addition to his teaching duties, he did extensive research. This included performing repeated human dissections, through which he hoped to better understand the flow of blood through the body.

At the time, nearly all doctors believed that Galen had explained the blood's movements and the heart's actions fairly satisfactorily. According to Galen, two kinds of blood existed in the body. The first, called "nutritive blood," was made in the liver and carried by the veins to the organs. The second, called "vital blood," was made in the heart and carried by the arteries. Moreover, Galen held that the heart sucked blood out of the veins, rather than pumping blood through the body.

Harvey finally concluded that Galen's conception of the heart and blood, though a valiant attempt to explain these things in his own day, was all wrong.

Instead, Harvey said, the blood circulates through the body in a closed, circular, repeating sequence, or loop. It travels through the veins to the heart, from there to the lungs, where it picks up oxygen, and then goes back to the heart, which pumps it throughout the body via the arteries. In his landmark treatise *On the Motion of the Heart and Blood in Animals* (1628), he stated:

> The blood passes through the lungs and heart by the force of the ventricles, and is sent for distribution to all parts of the body, where it makes its way into the veins [and] then flows by the veins from the circumference on every side to the center, from the lesser to the greater veins, and is by them finally discharged into the vena cava and right auricle of the heart. . . . It is absolutely necessary to conclude that the blood in the animal body is impelled in a circle, and is in a state of ceaseless motion; that this is the act or function which the heart performs by means of its pulse [pumping action]; and that it is the sole and only end of the motion and contraction of the heart.[42]

Some doctors and scientists immediately accepted Harvey's explanation of human circulation and began advocating that knowledge, including teaching it in schools. However, a considerable number of others remained skeptical, so it took decades for his ideas to be completely accepted. The main stumbling

In this seventeenth-century painting physician William Harvey gives a demonstration on the circulation of the blood. Harvey discovered that blood circulates through the body in a closed, circular, repeating sequence that passes through the heart and lungs.

block was that the means by which blood transferred from the arteries to the veins in the body's extremities was still unknown. The tiny vessels, called capillaries, that actually link the arteries and veins, were too small to be seen by the naked eye. Only when microscopes powerful enough to reveal the capillaries became available was blood circulation completely understood and Harvey proven correct once and for all.

The Optical Microscope

Revealing the existence of capillaries was only one of numerous ways the optical, or "light," microscope revolutionized science and human civilization in general. It particularly aided the field of medicine in the 1700s and beyond. Huge amounts of modern medical research, including the momentous germ theory of disease, were the direct results of the invention and steady improvement of the microscope during the Scientific Revolution.

Like the telescope, the optical microscope was not invented by a single person in a given place and time. Rather, the consensus of historians is that both simple microscopes (having one convex lens) and compound microscopes (with two or more lenses) were created independently by several individuals. It appears that a number of unidentified European spectacle makers experimented with simple microscopes in late medieval times. These were essentially smaller versions of today's magnifying glasses. For a long time it was thought that two Dutch spectacle makers, Hans Janssen and his son, Zacharias, made a more sophisticated compound scope in 1590. However, this claim is now in doubt, partly because it has been determined that Zacharias was not even born until 1590.

More certain is that Galileo built a crude compound microscope in 1609. Also, Dutch astronomer Christiaan Huygens made a two-lens scope a few decades later. It was Galileo's friend, German botanist Giovanni Faber, who in 1625 coined the term "microscope," from the Greek words *micron,* meaning "small," and *skopein,* meaning "to look at."

Most of the earliest microscopes, especially the simple ones having a single lens, were long viewed as novelties. Evidently, serious scientists did not recognize their potential for doing research. The man who brought these scopes to the attention of biologists and other scientists, and thereby came to be called the father of microscopy, was Anton (or Antoine) van Leeuwenhoek (LAY-ven-hook). Born in Holland in 1632, he owned and ran a dry goods store in the town of Delft and supplemented his income by doing surveying work.

Acceptance of Spontaneous Generation

When germs were first discovered during the Scientific Revolution, the general consensus of scientists was that these tiny creatures played no vital role in nature. Yet some naturally questioned how the creatures had come to be. Over time, a number of European researchers came to believe that germs, like many other small living things observed in various niches of nature, spring suddenly from nonliving matter. This theory is most commonly referred to as spontaneous generation. Part of the supposed proof for it was that maggots were always found in decaying meat and appeared to grow spontaneously from it. What was not known at that time was that maggots were so often found in rotting meat because flies earlier had laid eggs in the meat. It was not until the nineteenth and twentieth centuries that scientists learned that germs reproduce like other living things and spread from one place to another via animals, people, the wind, moving water, and so forth.

Leeuwenhoek's passionate hobby, grinding glass into fine, polished lenses and using them as magnifying glasses, eventually made him famous. The series of single-lens scopes he made over the course of nearly five decades were of very high quality and the best of them magnified images of objects three hundred times. That made them more powerful than even the best compound scopes of his era. The reason for this, modern experts speculate, may have been that his grinding and polishing process was far superior to the ones employed by other researchers. (Leeuwenhoek closely guarded the secret of the process, which remains uncertain to this day.)

The initial objects Leeuwenhoek observed through his instruments were common ones, such as insects, leaves, salt crystals, pepper grains, and his own hairs, blood, and semen. A careful researcher, he took exhaustive notes describing the magnified images. He also asked acquaintances who were better artists than he to look through the lenses and draw detailed pictures of what they saw.

Leeuwenhoek's "Little Beasties"

Between 1673 and 1676, Leeuwenhoek made what was to be his greatest discovery. Seemingly swimming in pond water, urine, and other liquids he stud-

Leeuwenhoek's first microscope was actually a finely ground glass lens inserted between two metal plates that magnified objects by three hundred times.

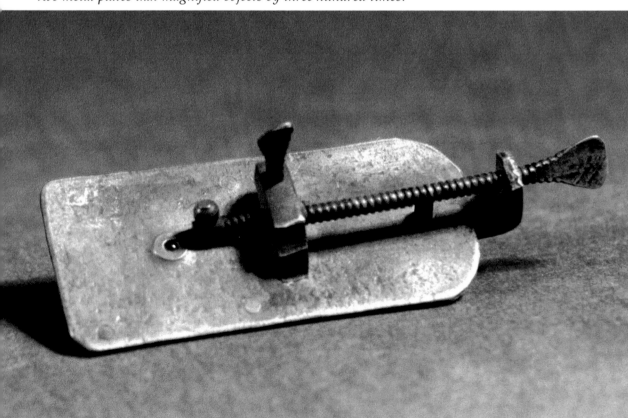

A Mouthful of Germs

Dutch store owner and amateur scientist Anton van Leeuwenhoek penned a number of descriptions of the "animalcules," or germs, he observed. This one was based on his study of scrapings from the mouth of a man who had never cleaned his teeth.

While I was talking to an old man . . . my eye fell upon his teeth, which were all coated over. So I asked him when he had last cleaned his mouth? And I got the answer that he'd never washed his mouth in all his life. So I took . . . some of the matter that was lodged between and against his teeth [i.e., plaque], and mixing it with his own spit, and also with fair water, [I] found an unbelievably great company of living animalcules, a-swimming more nimbly than any I had ever seen up to this time. The biggest sort (whereof there were a great plenty) bent their body into curves in going forward.

Quoted in Clifford Dobell. *Antony van Leeuwenhoek and His Little Animals.* New York: Dover, 1960, pp. 242–243.

ied were tiny creatures that were invisible to the unaided eye. He called them "animaicules," and later, in a more comical mood, "little beasties." As time went on, he found them in practically every material he viewed in his scopes, including food, human and animal wastes, the bodies of insects, and scrapings from people's teeth (including his own). Leeuwenhoek penned one of his descriptions of the creatures that would come to be called germs after examining some pond water in 1674:

The motion of most of these animalcules in the water was so swift, and so various, upwards, downwards, and round about, that 'twas wonderful to see. And I judge that some of these little creatures were above a thousand times smaller than the smallest ones I have ever yet seen, upon the rind of cheese.[43]

In 1683, after observing a host of germs in some scrapings taken from his own teeth, Leeuwenhoek wrote: "For my part, I judge [that] all the people living in our united Netherlands are not as many as the living animals that I carry in my own mouth this very day."[44] He recognized that knowledge of these tiny creatures might be important to science and wanted to share observations of them with the Royal Society. So, from 1674 until his death in 1723, Leeuwenhoek sent many letters to that London-based organization. In one of the first, he

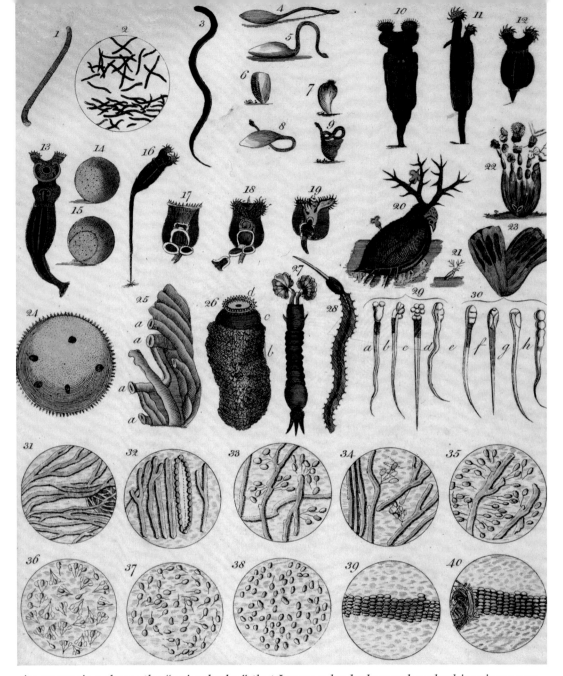

An engraving shows the "animalcules" that Leeuwenhoek observed under his microscope.

modestly said: "I beg you and the gentlemen under whose eyes this comes to bear in mind that my observations and opinions are only the result of my own impulse and curiosity. Take my simple pen, my boldness, and my opinions for what they are."[45]

At first, the scientists at the Royal Society were fascinated by Leeuwenhoek's claims about seeing minuscule animals in water and other substances. But they became disappointed and even somewhat suspicious when they could not replicate his experiments. During the later years of the Scientific Revolution, the Royal Society set a new standard. Its members demanded that any new scientific discovery must be verified by having other scientists repeat the experiment performed by the discoverer. If it could not be repeated, the reasoning went, it was likely not valid. (This standard remains a cornerstone of science today.)

Fortunately for Leeuwenhoek, English naturalist Robert Hooke (born 1635) was the society's curator of experiments. Over and over again, he kept trying to reproduce the Dutchman's conditions and technique using a scope of similar design and size. In November 1677, the tireless Hooke was finally successful and managed to see the germs for himself. The minutes of the society's next meeting said in part:

> Mr. Hooke had all this week discovered great numbers of exceedingly small animals swimming to and fro. They appeared of the bigness of a mite through a glass that magnified about [450 times]. They were observed to have all manner of motions to and fro in the water. And by all who saw them, they were verily believed to be animals. . . . They were seen by Sir Christopher Wren, Sir Jonas Moore, [and] diverse others, so that there was no longer any doubt of Mr. Leeuwenhoek's discovery.[46]

At the time, no one, including Hooke, his colleagues, and Leeuwenhoek himself, had any idea what the microscopic creatures were or how they had come into existence. It appeared to them that they were perfectly harmless, so they did not think to connect them to disease. In fact, the consensus of scientists was that the tiny animals served no specific purpose in nature (a supposition that would be found to be totally wrong about two centuries later).

Exquisite Beauty

In the meantime, the optical microscope remained a boon to scientists, both amateur and professional, during the final century of the Scientific Revolution. Leeuwenhoek continued to study all manner of objects, as did hundreds of other amateurs. (Among them were gentleman-scholars in Britain's American colonies, the future United States, where twenty-five colonists became members of the Royal Society.)

Also, Hooke constructed his own microscopes, with which he performed hundreds of experiments. His book *Micrographia* was intended to demonstrate to scientists and the public alike the potential use of the instrument in biology. It contained beautiful engravings (drawings) of many of the magnified images he had produced. Among them were a fly's compound eye, plant cells, and the bodies of lice, fleas, and other insects. (Hooke did many of his own drawings because he had earlier studied portrait painting in London.) Hooke's book and others like it became

Millions of Tiny Pores

This excerpt from Robert Hooke's Micrographia *describes his microscopic observation of tiny pores in burnt vegetable matter.*

Charcoal, or a vegetable burnt black, affords an object no less pleasant than instructive; for if you take a small round [piece of] charcoal and break it short with your fingers, you may perceive it to break with a very smooth and sleek surface. . . . This surface, if it be looked on with an ordinary microscope, does manifest [an] abundance of those pores which are also visible to the eye in many kinds of wood. . . . But this is not all, for besides those . . . if a better microscope be made use of, there will appear an infinite company of exceedingly small, and very regular pores. [These] were so exceeding small and thick, that in a line of them, 1/12th part of an inch long, I found by numbering them no less then 150, [and] therefore in a line of them an inch long, must be no less then 2,700 pores, and in a circular area of an inch diameter, must be about 5,725,350 of [them], which would, I doubt not, seem even incredible, were not everyone left to believe his own eyes.

Robert Hooke. *Micrographia.* Part XVI. http:// home.clara.net/rod.beavon/micro_16.htm.

An illustration shows the compound microscope used by Robert Hooke in his research for his book Micrographia.

widely popular in large part because of such drawings. According to scholar Lisa Jardine:

> The tiny living organisms depicted in seventeenth-century scientific engravings appeared arrestingly strange and beautiful. When [one noted researcher] first looked at an insect through a lens, his immediate thought was to seek out the best contemporary artists to record the exquisite beauty of what he saw.[47]

These artistic renderings also inspired numerous individuals to become biologists and other scientists, another crucial contribution made by the microscope, which was largely a product of the Scientific Revolution.

Chapter Six

Newton and Universal Gravitation

One of the greatest achievements of the Scientific Revolution was the discovery of some of the major forces holding together and causing the motions of the stars, planets, and other objects making up the universe. Before that, no one knew for sure what kept Earth in orbit around the sun and the moon moving around Earth. Scientists and philosophers had offered educated guesses to explain such motions for a long time. In the ancient world, for example, Aristotle and Ptolemy had posited giant, invisible, rotating spheres that held the heavenly bodies and carried them along.

Many centuries later, Johannes Kepler, who had shown that the planets move in ellipses around the sun, thought that some sort of invisible force might be acting on these bodies. Just such an invisible force—magnetism—was known in his time. So he suggested that a magnetic-like force might be at work in the heav-

ens. "The machinery of the heavens," he said, is "like a clock [and] in it almost all the variety of motions is from one very simple magnetic force acting on bodies, as in the clock all motions are from a very simple weight."[48]

Later still, René Descartes, who contributed mightily to refining the scientific method, took a different approach. He proposed that the space between the heavenly bodies was filled with an invisible, flexible material that exerted pressure. That pressure held those bodies in their various places, he said.

However, in the last century of the Scientific Revolution these and other theories about the motions of the heavenly bodies were swept away. After English scientist Robert Boyle (born 1627) showed that a vacuum, or space having no air, could exist, researchers began to speculate that outer space was a giant vacuum. In time, that idea became increasingly accepted, and most scientists concluded that Descartes was likely wrong about his invisible material.

Also, English scientist Isaac Newton demonstrated that there was indeed a force that bound the planets to the sun and the moon to the earth. Only it was not related to magnetism. He called it gravity and his theory came to be called universal gravitation. Newton also worked out a set of universal laws of motion that could be applied to objects both on earth and in outer space.

In retrospect, these accomplishments established Newton as the greatest scientist not only of the Scientific Revolution but also before the twentieth century. As historian Margaret C. Jacob puts it, his

achievements were so important that they altered the Western understanding of nature profoundly. It became possible, indeed essential, to imagine nature bounded by laws that are knowable through experimentation and mathematical [explanation].[49]

The Apple, Moon, and Beyond

Newton's proposal that objects move the same way in the far reaches of the universe as they do on Earth seems simple and obvious today. However, it was an enormous revelation in his day. Before his time, most researchers assumed that whatever forces made earthly objects move and kept those objects firmly on Earth's surface were different and separate from the forces that made Earth move around the sun. Newton's first major feat was to show that the same force was at work on Earth and in the heavens. So that force—gravity—must be universal.

Newton claimed that his first important inklings about gravity came when he saw an apple fall from a tree. Like other scientists, he realized that the apple fell because some mysterious force pulled it and other earthly objects toward the planet's center. The question that started forming in his mind was how far, or over what distance, did that force continue to work? If he stood on the highest mountain on Earth and dropped an object, he reasoned, it would surely fall and strike the ground in the same way the apple fell from the tree. That indicated that the force was potent enough to work over distances of tens of thousands of feet. It seemed only logical to him, therefore, that it would do the same over thousands of miles as well.

Therefore, Newton surmised, the moon, which orbits Earth at a distance of a few hundred thousand miles, might be bound to Earth by the same force that worked on the apple. If so, the moon is "falling" toward Earth. The moon does not plunge right onto Earth, causing huge destruction, he realized, because the smaller body possesses a considerable forward motion. In the words of science historian Gale E. Christianson,

Envisioning the moon as a giant apple, Newton developed the idea of how gravity works. The satellite's tendency to move away from

Newton claimed that he first started thinking about gravity when he observed an apple falling from a tree. He substituted the apple for the moon and came up with his theories about gravity.

earth in a straight line is counteracted by the inward pull of gravity, which produces an orbit, much as an object on a string when it is whirled around one's head. The moon is perfectly balanced between the tendency to move outward—or what is termed centrifugal force—and the inward [gravitational] pull of earth.[50]

Likewise, Newton reasoned, the sun's gravity attracts Earth and the other planets. These bodies are inclined to fall toward the sun as a result, but their forward motions cancel out gravity's pull and keep them in orbit around the larger, brightly shining object. Furthermore, Newton concluded, gravity must work in the very same manner throughout the known universe. To demonstrate this, he developed a neat, compact mathematical formula:

$$f = G\,\frac{m_1 \times m_2}{d^2}$$

Here, f stands for the force of attraction, or gravity, between two objects. The masses of the objects are designated m_1 and m_2 (which are multiplied by each other), and d is the distance between them (which is squared, or multiplied by itself). G is what Newton called the gravitational constant. That special figure, he determined, is the same, or remains constant, no matter which objects are plugged into the formula.

Using this equation, Newton showed, anyone could quite easily calculate the amount of attraction exerted by one object on another. One could also determine the masses of the objects in the solar system (the group of planets and other bodies orbiting the sun). For instance, knowing the distance between Earth and the moon, scientists later used Newton's formula to discover the masses of these bodies. Moreover, once these figures were known, they could calculate the sun's mass and from there, the masses of other planets. Mercury, the closest planet to the sun, was found to be one-twentieth as massive as Earth. Jupiter, the largest planet, turned out to be 318 times more massive than Earth. In this way, the theory of universal gravitation revolutionized science. Scholar John Gribbin writes that Newton

removed the mystery from the behavior of heavenly bodies, and opened the eyes of scientists to the fact that the behavior of the stars and planets—the behavior of the whole

An Alternate View of Gravity

Although Newton showed conclusively that gravity exists, his description of objects exerting forces on one another turned out to be only one way of explaining how gravity works. In the early twentieth century, German scientist Albert Einstein offered a different view. He argued that gravity is not a property of objects, but of space itself. Einstein said that space is made of an invisible fabric with an elastic, or bendable, quality. Planets and other objects interact with this hidden fabric by sinking into it. Objects with little mass sink only a tiny bit, he said, while more massive ones create deeper depressions in the fabric. In this view, Earth appears to attract the moon because the smaller body rolls "downhill" into the depression created by the larger one. This corresponds to Earth "pulling on" the moon in Newtonian terms. (Fortunately, the moon's forward motion counteracts the fall and keeps it in orbit around Earth.) Modern scientists point out that Newton's formula for gravity works the same way and remains perfectly valid in Einstein's version of space.

universe—might be explained using the same laws of physics that are derived from studies carried out in laboratories on earth.[51]

Other Gravitational Calculations

Among these studies were all manner of mathematical formulas, calculations, and discoveries about the heavenly bodies that were directly or indirectly derived from Newton's theory of gravity. For example, researchers found that the formula for universal gravitation could be used to mathematically verify Kepler's laws of planetary motion. Kepler had derived those laws directly, by correlating Tycho Brahe's mass of observations of the planets' yearly motions. In contrast, Newton's formula derived the same laws indirectly, solely through mathematics. Two divergent paths had therefore been used to reach the same astronomical destination.

Scientists also found that they could use Newton's formula to find out the strength of gravity's pull on Earth's surface and the surfaces of other worlds as well. One's weight on those worlds could then be calculated, too. The more massive the body, of course, the larger its gravity will be and vice versa. So one would expect to weigh less on a planet less massive than Earth and weigh more on a planet more massive than Earth.

This is exactly what experts found using formulas derived from Newton's. As an example, they showed that a person who weighs 160 pounds (73kg)

on Earth will weigh only 26 pounds (11.7kg) on the moon. This is because the moon's mass is much smaller than that of Earth, and therefore a person standing on the moon weighs 17 percent, or a bit more than one-sixth, of what he or she does on Earth. Using the same formula, one finds that the same 160-pound person would weigh 60 pounds (27kg) on Mars, 378 pounds (172kg) on Jupiter, and 4,331 pounds (1965kg) on the sun. (Keep in mind that Jupiter and the sun are gaseous bodies. So they have no solid surfaces to stand on.)

Still another implication of universal gravitation derived from Newton's formula is the phenomenon known as escape velocity, which comes into play when using rockets to carry objects into space. Escape velocity is the speed an object needs to move in order to escape the gravity of another object. For example, Earth's escape velocity is roughly 7 miles per second (11.265km per second). In other words, a rocket must attain that speed to break free of the gravitational attraction exerted by the planet.

In comparison, imagine trying to launch a rocket from the surface of the planet Neptune (if it had a solid surface). Neptune is more massive than Earth. So one would need to attain a higher escape velocity to break free of Neptune's gravitational pull. The highest escape velocity in the solar system is that of the sun—about 385 miles per second (619.6km per second). By contrast, Earth's moon has an escape velocity of only 1.5 miles per second (2.41km per second). That means that the American astronauts who visited the moon in 1969 had an easier time getting off the moon than they had earlier when leaving Earth.

Newton Explains Motion

Gravity is not the only universal property of the stars, planets, and other objects making up the cosmos, Newton pointed out. All of those objects, whether near or far from Earth, move through space, he said. Moreover, there must be universal laws that govern those motions. He derived three such basic laws, which he published, along with his ideas about gravity, in his 1687 work the *Principia.* (The latter is the commonly used short name for the book's full Latin title—*Philosophiæ Naturalis Principia Mathematica,* or *Mathematical Principles of Natural Philosophy* in English.)

The first of the three laws of motion Newton introduced deals with the phenomenon of inertia, the tendency of objects to resist change. In order for an object to move, he said, some kind of outside force must push or pull on it, because if that did not happen the object would remain motionless, or at rest. His law of inertia states that such an object will either stay at rest or move in a straight line at a steady rate of speed unless acted on by an outside force. According to veteran science explainer Andrew Rader:

If nothing is happening to you, and nothing does happen, you will never go anywhere. If you're going in a specific direction, unless something happens to you, you will

always go in that direction, forever. You can see good examples of this idea when you see video footage of astronauts. Have you ever noticed that their tools float? They can just place them in space and they stay in one place. There is no interfering force to cause this situation to change. The same is true when they throw objects for the camera. Those objects move in a straight line. If they threw something when doing a space-walk, that object would continue moving in the same direction and with the same speed unless interfered with, for example, if a planet's gravity pulled on it.[52]

Newton's basic laws on motion and gravity were published in his monumental 1687 work the Principia.

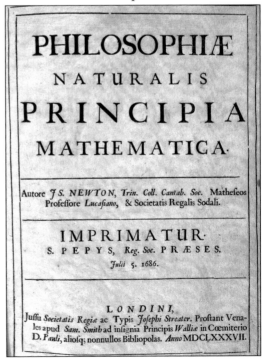

The Great Ocean of Truth

Even in his own time Isaac Newton was widely recognized as one of the most brilliant individuals who ever lived. Yet he recognized that he had only barely scratched the surface of the huge amount of knowledge about the universe that actually exists. In that regard, one of his most famous statements showed remarkable humbleness. Not long before his death in 1727, at age eighty-four, he told a contemporary biographer,

I do not know what I may appear to the world, but to myself I seem to have been only a boy playing on the sea-shore, and diverting myself in now and then finding a smoother pebble or a prettier shell than ordinary, while the great ocean of truth lay all undiscovered before me.

From "Memorable Quotes and Quotations from Isaac Newton." www.memorable-quotes.com/isaac+newton,a1100.html.

Newton's second law of motion deals with the nature and size of the forces that might act to make an object move. Essentially, it says that such a force will do one or more of three things to an object—speed it up, or accelerate it; slow it down, or decelerate it; or alter the direction in which the object is moving. Much of what happens depends on the object's mass. Obviously, the greater the mass, the stronger the force needed to accelerate it, decelerate it, or change its direction of motion.

A good example of the second law is what happens when someone fires a cannon. One force, the gunpowder explosion in the rear of the cannon, causes the stationary cannonball to accelerate. If someone fired the cannon in outer space, in a region far away from planets and other bodies exerting gravity, the ball would, as stated in the first law, keep on moving along in a straight line. But if the cannon is fired on Earth (or some other large body), a second force, gravity, soon acts on the moving ball in two ways. First, it causes it to decelerate, and, second, it makes the ball move downward in a curved arc toward the ground.

The ball's mass also comes into play in such a case. If it weighs 20 pounds (9kg), the explosion will propel it a certain distance before gravity pulls it to the ground. On the other hand, if the ball weighs 50 pounds (22.6kg), the same explosion will propel it a considerably shorter distance before gravity decelerates it and pulls it downward.

Newton's third law of motion deals with an important consequence of an object's motion—that the force causing that motion must be matched by a second force. Simply stated, the third law says that for every action there is an equal and opposite reaction. One way of looking at this situation is that forces occur in pairs. "Think about the time you sit in a chair," Rader writes.

> Your body exerts a force downward and that chair needs to exert an equal force [contained in the strength of its materials] upward or the chair will collapse. It's an issue of symmetry. Acting forces encounter other forces in the opposite direction. There's also the example of shooting a cannonball. When the cannonball is fired through the air (by the explosion), the cannon is pushed backward. The force pushing the ball out was equal to the force pushing the cannon back, but the effect on the cannon is less noticeable because it has a much larger mass.[53]

A man pushes a lawnmower to demonstrate Newton's laws of motion. The first law states that an object will either remain at rest or move at a continuous speed, unless acted on by force.

Boyle's Silent Void

The idea that a vacuum, or empty void, could not exist in nature was advocated by numerous ancient thinkers, as well as many early modern scientists. They believed that outer space was filled with an invisible material that many called the ether. But one of the greatest researchers of the Scientific Revolution, Robert Boyle, proved that a vacuum could *exist by pumping the air out of a glass container. In the years that followed, several other scientists suggested that a large-scale vacuum might exist in outer space. If so, it was a silent void, for one of Boyle's experiments showed that sound cannot travel in a vacuum. One expert observer puts it this way:*

In outer space, sound would need something to carry it. The scientist Robert Boyle discovered this in 1660. He made an experiment by placing his watch in a jar and then he pumped the air out. When he listened to the jar, he could not hear any sound coming from his watch. If you and a friend were on the moon and tried to talk to each other, you couldn't hear, unless you took along a walkie-talkie!

Jeanette Cain. "Sound and Air." www .light-science.com/soundair.html.

Robert Boyle, right, discusses with French scientist Denis Papin their 1675 experiments that used air pumps to create a vacuum within a glass container.

Another familiar example of Newton's third law in action is firing off a rocket. The force of the hot gases shooting backward from the rocket's lower end causes an equal amount of force in the opposite direction. This takes the form of the rocket's powerful forward motion.

"Let Newton Be"

Newton's *Principia* was in many ways the culmination of the Scientific Revolution. Nicolaus Copernicus, Tycho, Roger Bacon, Francis Bacon, Kepler, Galileo, and others had laid a firm foundation for him, hence his famous statement (in a letter to Robert Hooke), "If I have seen further, it is by standing on the shoulders of giants."[54] Despite his modesty, however, Newton had jumped proverbial light-years ahead of his predecessors and in so doing opened the way for the emergence of modern science.

Indeed, in the two and a half centuries following Newton's death (in 1727), science, especially the disciplines of physics, astronomy, mathematics, chemistry, and optics, changed human society in ways too numerous to list. Among the major ones, first, he finalized the scientific method initially developed by Ibn Alhazen, Galileo, the Bacons, and Descartes by showing how it could be consistently applied to complex theories in a wide range of scientific disciplines. Even more significant, Newton revealed how the universe works, showing that a small set of basic mathematical laws can explain the motions of almost all the bodies in nature. That made it possible for later astronomers to form theories about the origins and structure of the cosmos, which reached their height of success in the mid- to late twentieth century.

Newton also made it easier for astronomers, physicists, and other scientists to formulate and prove fresh theories by inventing a new, complex form of mathematics—calculus. (He was dubbed the cocreator of calculus with German mathematician Gottfried Leibniz.) In addition, Newton's equations and laws concerning gravity and motion made possible powered flight, which began in the early twentieth century. That rapidly led to airplanes of numerous types, rockets, and the advent of space travel and exploration.

It is no wonder that Newton's name has become synonymous with the Scientific Revolution and the development of modern science. In a eulogy given at his funeral, noted English poet Alexander Pope beautifully and aptly summed up the debt humanity owed Newton. His voice breaking with emotion, Pope said, "Nature and nature's laws lay hid in night. God said 'Let Newton be!' And all was light."[55]

The Enlightenment and Beyond

It has been established that the Scientific Revolution's principal legacy to humanity was to create the fertile soil from which modern science grew. In addition, it produced another crucial legacy that was not strictly about science. Namely, the scientific movement that culminated in Newton and his profound concepts inspired the European Enlightenment. The Enlightenment was a mainly eighteenth-century intellectual movement initially spearheaded by liberal English and French thinkers. Over time its ideas spread to England's North American colonies, where Thomas Jefferson, Benjamin Franklin, and other colonial leaders absorbed them.

Put simply, the Enlightenment could not have come about without the Scientific Revolution. Before the latter, most thinkers in Europe and elsewhere did not challenge tradition, especially the teachings and rules of religion. In Europe, the church strongly advocated acceptance of ancient authorities like Aristotle. It discouraged new ideas and experimentation and promoted maintaining the intellectual status quo. The mysteries of nature were for God, not humans, to know, church leaders said, and people should not tamper in the Creator's domain.

Nicolaus Copernicus, Galileo, and Isaac Newton challenged this conventional thinking and showed that human reason and new explorations of nature's mysteries could exist hand in hand with religious faith. "Just as important," one modern observer points out, "Newton [and his immediate predecessors] showed that scientific thought and methods could be applied to nonscientific topics—a development that paved the way for numerous later thinkers of the Enlightenment."[56]

These Enlightenment thinkers also challenged tradition and the authority of the church. For the most part, however, the new movement applied human reason to society in general rather than to science alone. This approach was intended in part to make society better and more humane, and also to foster liberty, for both individuals and entire nations. As noted historian Donald Kagan explains, the Enlightenment's leading voices

> combined confidence in the human mind inspired by the Scientific Revolution and faith in the power of rational criticism to challenge the intellectual authority of tradition and the Christian past. These writers stood convinced that human beings could comprehend the operation of physical nature and mold it to the ends of material and moral improvement. The rationality of the physical universe became a standard against which the customs and traditions of society could be measured and criticized. Such criticism penetrated every corner of contemporary society, politics, and religious opinion. As a result, the spirit of innovation and improvement came to characterize European and Western society.[57]

America's Founding Fathers were profoundly influenced by the liberal English and French thinkers of the Age of Enlightenment.

Rejecting the Intolerant Past

The spirit of fresh innovation and of trying to improve society during each succeeding generation was a bold step forward for Western civilization. In the eighteenth century, with the Enlightenment, Europe began to separate itself from the more primitive, superstitious, intolerant worldview it had been mired in during medieval times. Its leading thinkers and educators strove to become more open minded, thoughtful, learned, progressive, and humane; in other words, more *enlightened.*

Among the core concepts of the new enlightened worldview was the realization that nature works by scientific principles, an idea that had come straight out of the Scientific Revolution. Other major concepts of the Enlightenment included rejection of superstition and fears of the unknown; religious tolerance; the notion that human understanding comes from experience, or trying new ways of doing things; and acceptance of the idea that exploring new paths is superior to blindly following authority. Washington State University scholar Richard Hooker cites a few other central tenets of Enlightenment thinking:

All human life, both social and individual, can be understood in the same way the natural world can be understood. Once understood, human life, both social and individual, can be manipulated or engineered in the same way the natural world can be manipulated or engineered. Human history is largely a history of progress. [And] human beings can be improved through education and the development of their rational facilities.[58]

From Scientific Reason to Democracy

Perhaps the most important of all the products of Enlightenment thought was the idea that certain basic, natural human rights exist and that these should be respected by governments and the church. In England, France, and the American colonies in particular, leading thinkers and legislators came to believe that humans should make both society and governments fairer and more equitable and just. The way to achieve this noble aim, they said, was to begin promoting and implementing basic human rights. These included freedom of thought, freedom of self-expression (or speech), freedom of association and public assembly, and freedom to choose or dispose of one's leaders.

These were some of the fundamental concepts that inspired Jefferson and his colleagues to break away from Britain and establish a new nation, the United States. The U.S. Founding Fathers were influenced by numerous earlier thinkers, writers, and political innovators, but they were especially inspired by the chief writers of the Enlightenment, particularly Englishman John Locke. He advocated that kings and other absolute rulers—whose rule had been the norm for untold ages—almost always curbed

In Two Treatises of Government *John Locke wrote that government should be fashioned by and subject to the will of the people and that the principal duty of governments was to protect the civil rights of the citizenry.*

their subjects' basic human rights. In his masterwork, *Two Treatises of Government* (1690), Locke said that politics and government in a nation should not be manipulated and controlled by a monarch who does as he or she pleases and answers to no one. Instead, a government should be fashioned by and subject to the will of the people who are governed. Equally important, the principal duty of those who run a government must be to protect the civil rights of the citizenry. "No one ought to harm another in his life, health, liberty, or possessions," Locke insisted.

And that all men may be restrained from invading others' rights and from doing hurt to one another, and the law of nature be observed . . . the execution of the law of nature is, in that state, put into every man's hands [i.e., the people should rule]. In transgressing the law of nature, the offender declares himself to live by another rule than that of reason and common equity; which is that measure God has set to the actions of men for their mutual security.[59]

Using such ideas borrowed from Locke and other Enlightenment thinkers, Jefferson, Franklin, and the other U.S. founders created the first modern democracy. In time, its concepts of liberty, equality, and government by and for the people (coupled with similar ideas promoted by the French Revolution in 1789) spread across the world. This was the extraordinary end product of a series of revolutions in human thought, each erected upon those that preceded it. The Scientific Revolution, born from the brains of a few dynamic, industrious individuals, promoted the idea that the human mind is capable of unlocking nature's secrets. That inspired the Enlightenment, with its concept that every person has worth and dignity and possesses fundamental rights. The next, logical step was the instigation of working democracies, which are still in the process of reshaping the human condition. Despite their soaring intellects, Copernicus, Galileo, and their fellow scientific revolutionaries were not able to foresee the monumental chain of world-altering events they had set in motion.

Notes

Introduction: To Create a Better World

1. Margaret C. Jacob. *The Scientific Revolution: A Brief History with Documents.* New York: St. Martin's, 2010, p. 1.
2. Steven Shapin. *The Scientific Revolution.* Chicago: University of Chicago Press, 1996, p. 7.
3. Jacob. *The Scientific Revolution,* p. 3.
4. Robert K. Merton. *Social Theory and Social Structure.* New York: Free Press, 1968, pp. 671–672.
5. Lisa Jardine. *Ingenious Pursuits: Building the Scientific Revolution.* New York: Doubleday, 1999, p. 363.

Chapter One: Forerunners of Modern Science

6. Rex Warner. *The Greek Philosophers.* New York: New American Library, 1972, pp. 9–10.
7. Aristotle. *Metaphysics* and *On the Heavens,* quoted in Philip Wheelwright, ed. *The Presocratics.* New York: Macmillan, 1987, pp. 46–47.
8. Lucretius. *The Nature of the Universe.* Translated by Ronald Latham. New York: Penguin, 1994, p. 197.
9. Quoted in Wheelwright. *The Presocratics,* pp. 160–161.
10. John Gribbin. *The Fellowship: Gilbert, Bacon, Harvey, Wren, Newton, and the Story of the Scientific Revolution.* New York: Overlook, 2007, p. 24.

11. Gribbin. *The Fellowship,* p. 24.
12. Quoted in James Reston Jr. *Galileo: A Life.* New York: HarperCollins, 1994, p. 9.
13. Shapin. *The Scientific Revolution,* pp. 75–76.
14. Jacob. *The Scientific Revolution,* pp. 6–7.

Chapter Two: The Sun-Centered Universe

15. Angus Armitage. *The World of Copernicus.* New York: New World Library, 1972, pp. 58–59.
16. Aristotle. "On the Heavens," in Jonathan Barnes, ed. *The Complete Works of Aristotle.* Vol. 1. Princeton, NJ: Princeton University Press, 1984, p. 489.
17. Nicolaus Copernicus. *On the Revolutions of the Heavenly Spheres.* Translated by Charles G. Wallace. Chicago: Encyclopedia Britannica, 1952, p. 519.
18. Copernicus. *On the Revolutions of the Heavenly Spheres,* p. 519.
19. Nicolaus Copernicus. *On the Revolutions.* Translated by Edward Rosen. Baltimore: Johns Hopkins University Press, 1992, p. 38.
20. Quoted in John L.E. Dreyer. *A History of Astronomy from Thales to Kepler.* New York: Dover, 1953, p. 315.
21. Thomas S. Kuhn. *The Copernican Revolution: Planetary Astronomy in the Development of Western Thought.* New York: MJF, 1985, p. 144.

22. Quoted in Galileo Galilei. *Le Opere di Galileo Galilei*. Vol. 10. Edited by Antonio Favaro. Florence, Italy: G. Barbera Editrice, 1968, p. 68.
23. Giordano Bruno. *The Ash Wednesday Supper*. Translated by Stanley L. Jaki. www.math.dartmouth.edu/~matc/Readers/renaissance.astro/6.1.Supper.html.
24. From "Quotations by Johannes Kepler." Translated by J.V. Field. www-history.mcs.st-and.ac.uk/Quotations/Kepler.html.

Chapter Three: An Eye on the Sky: The Telescope

25. Shapin. *The Scientific Revolution*, pp. 19–20.
26. Quoted in John R. Christianson. *On Tycho's Island: Tycho Brahe and His Assistants, 1570–1601*. New York: Cambridge University Press, 2000, pp. 22–23.
27. Quoted in Gilbert Scatterthwaite. "Did the Reflecting Telescope Have English Origins?" www.chocky.demon.co.uk/oas/diggeshistory.html.
28. James MacLachlan. *Galileo Galilei: First Physicist*. New York: Oxford University Press, 1997, p. 50.
29. Quoted in Giorgio de Santillana. *The Crime of Galileo*. Chicago: University of Chicago Press, 1955, p. 9.
30. Quoted in Gale E. Christianson. *Isaac Newton and the Scientific Revolution*. New York: Oxford University Press, 1996, p. 51.
31. Quoted in Michael Hunter. *Science and the Shape of Orthodoxy*. New York: Boydell, 1995, p. 55.

Chapter Four: The Scientific Method Advances

32. Aristotle. *Posterior Analytics*, in *The Complete Works of Aristotle*. Vol. 1, p. 150.
33. H.D.P. Lee. Introduction to, *Meteorology*, by Aristotle. Cambridge, MA: Harvard University Press, 1952, p. xxvii.
34. Jim Al-Khalili. "The First True Scientist." http://news.bbc.co.uk/2/hi/science/nature/7810846.stm.
35. Martyn Shuttleworth. "History of the Scientific Method." www.experiment-resources.com/history-of-the-scientific-method.html.
36. Roger Bacon. *On Experimental Science*. Internet Medieval Sourcebook. www.fordham.edu/halsall/source/bacon2.html.
37. Quoted in Jacob, *The Scientific Revolution*, pp. 74–75.

Chapter Five: The Revival of Medical Research

38. Arthur J. Brock. Introduction to *On the Natural Faculties*, by Galen. Translated by Arthur J. Brock. Chicago: Encyclopedia Britannica, 1952, p. ix.
39. Gribbin. *The Fellowship*, p. 94.
40. Gribbin. *The Fellowship*, p. 94.
41. Gribbin. *The Fellowship*, p. 95.
42. William Harvey. *On the Motion of the Heart and Blood in Animals*. Modern History Sourcebook. www.fordham.edu/halsall/mod/harvey-blood.html.
43. Quoted in Douglas Anderson. "Lens on Leeuwenhoek: The Letters, Period 1, 1673–1677." http://lensonleeuwenhoek.net/period1.htm.

44. Quoted in Theodor Rosebury. *Life on Man.* New York: Viking, 1969, p. 9.

45. Quoted in Jardine. *Ingenious Pursuits,* p. 90.

46. Quoted in Thomas Birch. *History of the Royal Society.* Vol. 3. London: A. Millar, 1756–1757, p. 352.

47. Jardine. *Ingenious Pursuits,* pp. 101–102.

Chapter Six: Newton and Universal Gravitation

48. From "Quotations by Johannes Kepler."

49. Jacob. *The Scientific Revolution,* p. 95.

50. Christianson. *Isaac Newton and the Scientific Revolution,* p. 39.

51. John Gribbin. *In Search of the Edge of Time: Black Holes, White Holes, and Wormholes.* New York: Penguin, 1999, p. 9.

52. Andrew Rader. "Newton's Laws of Motion." Physics4kids.com. www.physics4kids.com/files/motion_laws.html.

53. Rader. "Newton's Laws of Motion."

54. From "Memorable Quotes and Quotations from Isaac Newton." www.memorable-quotes.com/isaac+newton,a1100.html.

55. Quoted in "Sir Isaac Newton: Legacy of the Scientific Revolution, Conclusion." http://quazen.com/reference/biography/sir-isaac-newton-legacy-of-the-scientific-revolution/5/.

Epilogue: The Enlightenment and Beyond

56. SparkNotes Editors. "The Enlightenment (1650–1800)." www.sparknotes.com/history/european/enlightenment/section1.html.

57. Donald Kagan et al. *The Western Heritage, 1300–1815.* New York: Macmillan, 1983, p. 619.

58. Richard Hooker. "Seventeenth Century Enlightenment Thought." www.wsu.edu/~dee/ENLIGHT/ENLIGHT.HTM.

59. John Locke. *The Second Treatise of Government.* Edited by Thomas P. Peardon. Indianapolis: Bobbs-Merrill, 1952, p. 4.

Glossary

armillary: An astronomical device consisting of a framework of metal rings, used in naked-eye astronomy to observe the heavenly bodies.

atomic theory: The idea that all matter is made up of tiny particles called atoms.

capillaries: The tiny blood vessels linking the veins to the arteries in the bodies of animals and people.

compound microscope: A microscope consisting of two or more lenses.

cosmic: Having to do with the cosmos.

cosmos: The universe.

elliptical: Oval-shaped.

Enlightenment: A largely eighteenth-century European intellectual movement that advocated scientific exploration, religious toleration, human progress, and basic human rights.

escape velocity: The speed that a body needs to attain in order to escape the gravity of another body.

geocentric: Earth-centered.

gravitational constant: As determined by Isaac Newton, a special mathematical figure that always remains the same in his formula for gravity.

gravity: A universal force of attraction between one object and another.

heliocentric: Sun-centered.

heresy: Words or actions that contradict established beliefs or traditions, especially religious ones.

humanism: A movement in the early European Renaissance, the members of which advocated the worth, dignity, and intellectual powers of human beings.

hypothesis: A suggested idea or explanation that remains unproven.

inertia: The tendency of an object to remain either at rest or in motion unless affected by an outside force.

maria: Supposed "seas" on the moon, which are now known to be vast plains of dust.

mass: The total amount of matter making up an object.

naked-eye astronomy: Observations of the heavens before the invention of the telescope.

naturalist: A thinker or scientist interested in explaining the workings of nature.

physis: In ancient Greek science, nature's main underlying principle.

planet: A large, spherical object that usually orbits a star and shines by reflected light.

reductionism: The process of breaking down a whole into its constituent, or basic, parts.

reflector (or reflecting telescope): A telescope in which light bounces off a mirror and then passes through a lens to create a magnified image.

refractor (or refracting telescope): A telescope in which light passes through two lenses to create a magnified image.

revolve: To move around, as in Earth moving around the sun.

scientific method: A practical approach to doing scientific research.

secular: Nonchurch, or nonreligious.

simple microscope: A microscope consisting of a single lens.

solar system: The sun and all the planets, moons, asteroids, and other objects held by the sun's gravity.

star: A large heavenly body, like the sun, that shines by its own light as a result of continuous nuclear reactions taking place in its center.

syllogism: An exercise in logic that makes conclusions based on comparisons of various things.

theory: In science, a set of observations and facts that together appear to satisfactorily explain a given phenomenon.

treatise: A book or major study of something.

Tychonic model: The theory proposed by early modern Danish astronomer Tycho Brahe that suggested that the other planets revolved around the sun while the sun revolved around Earth.

universal gravitation: The theory of gravity proposed by Isaac Newton.

universe: The sum total of all the space and matter known to exist.

Western: European-based.

For More Information

Books

Asger Aaboe. *Episodes from the Early History of Astronomy.* New York: Springer, 2001. A valuable examination of several historical moments in science.

David Berlinski. *Newton's Gift: How Sir Isaac Newton Unlocked the System of the World.* New York: Free Press, 2000. One of the more easily readable explanations of Isaac Newton's discoveries and theories.

William J. Boerst. *Tycho Brahe: Mapping the Heavens.* Greensboro, NC: Morgan Reynolds, 2003. Written for middle school students, this volume nicely summarizes Tycho's many important accomplishments.

Gale E. Christianson. *Isaac Newton and the Scientific Revolution.* New York: Oxford University Press, 1996. An easy-to-read overview of Isaac Newton's work by an author twice nominated for the Pulitzer Prize.

Matthew Cobb. *Generation: The Seventeenth-Century Scientists Who Unraveled the Secrets of Sex, Life, and Growth.* New York: Bloomsbury, 2006. An excellent summary of several of the leading figures of the Scientific Revolution.

Nicholas Copernicus. *On the Revolutions.* Translated by Edward Rosen. Baltimore: Johns Hopkins University Press, 1992. The groundbreaking work advocating the sun-centered universe, which greatly inspired Galileo and was eventually banned by the church.

Stillman Drake. *Galileo.* New York: Sterling, 2010. An excellent short overview of Galileo's scientific contributions, written by the leading Galileo scholar of the twentieth century.

Joshua Gilder and Anne-Lee Gilder. *Heavenly Intrigue: Johannes Kepler, Tycho Brahe, and the Murder Behind One of History's Greatest Scientific Discoveries.* New York: Doubleday, 2004. This fascinating volume summarizes Tycho's and Kepler's contributions to science while exploring the theory that Kepler may have murdered Tycho.

John Gribbin. *The Fellowship: Gilbert, Bacon, Harvey, Wren, Newton, and the Story of the Scientific Revolution.* New York: Overlook, 2007. One of the better books about the Scientific Revolution, this covers all the major researchers that contributed to it.

Deborah E. Harkness. *The Jewel House: Elizabethan London and the Scientific Revolution.* New Haven, CT: Yale University Press, 2007. Harkness describes the major English contributors to the Scientific Revolution in a lively style that makes for easy but very informative reading.

Nigel Henbest. *DK Space Encyclopedia.* London: Dorling Kindersley, 1999. This critically acclaimed book is the best general source available for younger readers about the wonders of space.

Margaret C. Jacob. *The Scientific Revolution: A Brief History with Documents.* New York: St. Martin's, 2010. An excellent and accessible book that first gives a brief overview of the subject and then follows up with short readings by the major scientists of the era described.

Lisa Jardine. *Ingenious Pursuits: Building the Scientific Revolution.* New York: Doubleday, 1999. A well-researched and well-written volume that covers most major aspects of the subject.

Thomas S. Kuhn. *The Copernican Revolution: Planetary Astronomy in the Development of Western Thought.* New York: MJF, 1985. Kuhn, a noted American scientist, was famous for arguing that science progresses in a revolutionary process.

James MacLachlan. *Galileo Galilei: First Physicist.* New York: Oxford University Press, 1999. A brief but well-written and informative look at Galileo's scientific discoveries and trial.

William R. Newman. *Atoms and Alchemy: Chemistry and the Experimental Origins of the Scientific Revolution.* Chicago: University of Chicago Press, 2006. Newman describes several of the major experiments performed during the Scientific Revolution.

Natalie M. Rosinsky. *Sir Isaac Newton: Brilliant Mathematician and Scientist.* Minneapolis: Compass Point, 2008. A clearly written, informative biography of Newton, including how he formulated his famous theory of gravity.

George Saliba. *Islamic Science and the Making of the European Renaissance.* Cambridge, MA: MIT Press, 2007. Explains how Muslim thinkers influenced early European scientists.

Steven Shapin. *The Scientific Revolution.* Chicago: University of Chicago Press, 1996. A solid general overview of the subject.

William Sheehan. *Worlds in the Sky: Planetary Discovery from the Earliest Times Through* Voyager *and* Magellan. Tucson: University of Arizona Press, 1997. Chronicles some of the early pioneers of astronomy and explains their discoveries in a simple, clear manner.

Mitchell Young. *Scientific Revolution.* San Diego: Greenhaven Press, 2005. Aimed at young adults, this summary of the Scientific Revolution covers most of the major thinkers and their ideas.

Websites

Facts About Telescopes (www.meade.com.support/telewrk.html). This site, provided by Meade, one of the most reputable telescope manufacturers, explains in basic terms (aided by diagrams) how telescopes work.

History of Anatomy (www.historyworld.net/wrldhis/PlainTextHistories.asp?ParagraphID=akz1). This excellent site covers Vesalius, Harvey, and other pioneers of the study of the human body.

History of the Microscope (http:// inventors.about.com/od/mstart inventions/a/microscope.htm). A brief but useful overview of the early development of optical microscopes.

Intellectual History in the High Middle Ages (http://cliojournal.wikispaces .com/Intellectual+Activity+in+the +High+Middle+Ages). Covers the major thinkers of this crucial period in Europe's development.

The Islamic Golden Age and the Abbasids (www.muslims.eu/The_Islamic_ Golden_Age.html). An overview of the many and important accomplishments of Muslim scientists during a period when Europe had developed few significant thinkers of its own.

The Trial of Galileo (www.law.umkc .edu/faculty/projects/ftrials/gali leo/galileo.html). A useful collection of some of the main documents associated with Galileo's confrontation with the Inquisition.

Tycho Brahe (www.hps.cam.ac.uk/star ry/tycho.html). A useful summary of the achievements of the last great naked-eye astronomer.

Index

Picture Credits

About the Author

In addition to his numerous acclaimed volumes on ancient civilizations, historian Don Nardo has published several studies of scientific discoveries and phenomena. Among these are *The Extinction of the Dinosaurs, Polar Explorations, Black Holes, Extraterrestrial Life, Comets and Asteroids, Volcanoes, Climate Change,* and biographies of the noted scientists Tycho Brahe and Charles Darwin. Nardo also composes and arranges orchestral music. He lives with his wife, Christine, in Massachusetts.